Praise for *The Woods of Wicomico*

"Children will be captivated when they meet Timothy the tortoise, Octavious the osprey, Grahame the groundhog and their friends of various species, all dwelling in the woods of Wicomico. Nuala Galbari has written, and Buttons Boggs has illustrated, a narrative that's up-to-the minute in its environmental message, but timeless in its ability to bring animals to vital life as distinct individuals. Best of all, through its sparkling vocabulary, and original songs and lyrics, this book invites an engaged and creative response on the part of its young readers."
— Barbara J. King, author of *Being with Animals*

"Nuala Galbari's *The Woods of Wicomico* is a winner out of the gate. It expresses her powerful concern for the Chesapeake Bay environment, and is alive with endearing and expertly animated wildlife characters. The poem *Victus Astrum (Shining Star)* can easily bring a tear of concern and the awareness for action to the heart and mind of anyone reading this excellent book. Children will love it. I truly hope Nuala will consider expanding her effort into a powerful series covering the full ecosystem."
— Jim Welch, CEO
   IPAC Marine Environmental Research Corp,
   (a concerned nonprofit corporation)

"As a parent and grandparent reading The Woods of Wicomico to a young child, one soon begins to relive one's own childhood. The cast of animal characters become real as they plan on recovering their woodland home, causing one to ponder the fate of our own wild woodlands today – indeed the very fate of our planet - as we face increasing pollution and overpopulation. The Woods of Wicomico is a book not only for tomorrow's generation of occupants – our children and grandchildren – but also for us as adults. What are we to learn from the voices of Wicomico's animals? Such abstract concepts as time, duty and responsibility, as taught by old Cornelius the crow to Timothy Trumble the tortoise, apply to all of us today.
Only we can make this, our Earth, a better place."
— David L. Justis, M.D., Ph.D

"The author has woven together a story combining wit, charm and imagination with the rich natural abundance of Virginia's Bay and woodlands. She imbues a deep sense of place to this small patch of woods, rooted in nature and history, and crafts a compelling and timely message about protecting these special places before they are lost. Though intended as a children's story, it embraces themes of connections with nature and our past that we should all appreciate, and does so with elegant prose and lavish illustrations that everyone can enjoy."
— Thane Harpole, co-director, Fairfield Foundation

"Animal lore guarantees a flight-path into any child's heart and imagination, and Nuala Galbari and Buttons Boggs have, through the artful interweaving of narrative, song and illustration, provided a fanciful passage connecting sky, sea and land in an entertaining force of nature. No child

should be denied the opportunity of meeting the wondrous allegorical community of Wicomico, and as the reader is swept along on a mission to save the woods of Wicomico, we discover the environs of York River and Chesapeake Bay playing an equally central role in the drama. Ms. Galbari proves a consummate fablist delivering a story rich in simple metaphor, positioning markers of moral direction at comprehensible levels for even the youngest of readers. *The Woods of Wicomico* is reason enough to celebrate as the spirit of Potter, Aesop and Orwell live on in Ms. Galbari and her meaningful menagerie!"
— Phillip M. Church, Assoc. Professor, Dept of Theatre, Florida International University

To my barn buddy, Margaret, with love –

The Woods of Wicomico

— for the animals,

Nuala

The Woods

Rupert's Cadets
Ringbilled Gulls
Boot Camp

the Venerable Red Oak

Wouldn't this be a great place for pony pasture?

Octavia's

Cornelius's

Timothy's path

Turtle Beach

Rachel's Route to

Muskrat Lodge

Blue Heron Rookery

The Solaris

N W E S

The York River

Mattaponi & Pamunkey Rivers

to Chesapeake Bay

buttons

The Woods of Wicomico

Story, Music and Lyrics by Nuala C. Galbari
Illustrated by Buttons Boggs

Brandylane Publishers, Inc

Copyright 2010 by Nuala C. Galbari. No portion of this work may be reproduced in any form whatsoever without written permission from the publisher.

ISBN 978-1-883911-97-3

Library of Congress Control Number: 2010930163

Brandylane Publishers, Inc.
www.brandylanepublishers.com

Printed on recycled paper.

Printed in the United States of America

*For my parents
and Aunt Ada*

*and for Reginald Corvus
whose wings are now folded
but whose spirit lives on
in my heart*

~ Nuala Galbari

*With love for Joy and Jeannie,
in memory of my dad,
and for Mr. Grriffin, of course*

~ Buttons Boggs

"I have noticed in my life that all men have a liking for some special animal, tree, plant, or spot of earth. If men would pay more attention to these preferences and seek what is best to do in order to make themselves worthy of that toward which they are so attracted, they might have dreams which would purify their lives. Let a man decide upon his favorite animal and make a study of it, learning its innocent ways. Let him learn to understand its sounds and motions. The animals want to communicate with man but Wakantanka does not intend they shall do so directly—man must do the greater part in securing an understanding."

>Brave Buffalo (late 19th century)
>Teton Sioux medicine man

Contents

One	Timothy Trumble Meets a Powhatan Corvid	1
Two	Grahame Conveys Disquieting News	9
Three	Rupert and the Flight Cadets	15
Four	Dispatching the Company	23
Five	Stowaways	27
Six	Arrival of the Apparatus	33
Seven	Assateague Island	41
Eight	Tarquin	47
Nine	Penelope	55
Ten	Mustering the Muskrats	61
Eleven	The Sub-Tropical Tempest	71
Twelve	Sebastian	81
Thirteen	Powhatan Past	89
Fourteen	Tea and Archaeology	97
Fifteen	Honored Visitors	105
Sixteen	Right of Passage	111
	Word List	126
	Latin Glossary	132

Acknowledgements

In writing *The Woods of Wicomico* I received assistance from many sources, people and institutions. I would like to express my gratitude to all who offered inspiration, advice, support and encouragement, without whom this book would not have been published, including:

Geff C. Galbari, Barbara J. King, Ph.D., Meredith Hogg, Joseph Filipowski, Jim Welch, Connie Stewart, Chip Croft, David Meredith, Sharon Owen, Sarah Hogg, Annie Tobey, Ruby Lee Norris, and Charlie Moores.

I am grateful to the following organizations:

Wildlife Rehabilitation & Release, Minnesota
Abingdon Animal Clinic
Mid-Atlantic Turtle and Tortoise Society
Kaleidoscope Fine & Performing Arts
Gallery at York Hall
Carrot Tree Restaurant, Yorktown
Best of British, Hampton
SEA-TV Film & Production Company
Marine Environmental Research Corporation
DATA Investigations
Chesapeake Bay Foundation

Virginia Indian Cultural Center
Virginia Living Museum
Virginia Institute of Marine Science
Be the Bay—Chesapeake Environmental
      Communications
Ware Academy
Fairfield Foundation
Rosewell Foundation, Inc.
Colonial Williamsburg Foundation
The Mariners' Museum

Special appreciation goes to Buttons Boggs for her lavish illustrations, to Alyssa Owens for her fine music transcription, and to Samuel "Running Deer" Opechancanoe McGowan and Susan McGowan for their suggestions and encouragement. To Timothy Seaman, who never ceases to inspire, and to Thane Harpole and David Brown.

For their guidance and backing from the book's conception to its publication, I am deeply grateful to David L. Justis, M.D., Ph.D, to Robert H. Pruett, editor-in-chief and publisher, and to John Wegg, Editor-in-Chief, *AIRWAYS* magazine, without whom this would not have been possible.

Finally, to the animals – tame and wild – who have inspired this story.

CHAPTER ONE
Timothy Trumble Meets a Powhatan Corvid

Timothy Trumble navigated a direct path toward a group of dandelions. The small tortoise moved with a decisive gait, anticipating the delectable green leaves ahead of him. The morning sun moved higher through the azure sky, and a cluster of bright white stratus clouds drifted, almost imperceptibly, toward the east. Timothy followed a wildlife trail, a well-used thoroughfare that made his travel somewhat easier than working his way through the blades of grass.

Suddenly, he was interrupted by a loud voice above him.

"No, no, no!" said the voice. "Not that way! *This* way!"

Timothy lifted his head a little to the left to see a rather large fish crow surveying him from a low branch on the tulip tree.

"If you please, how do you know where I'm going?" asked Timothy, quite politely.

The corvid studied Timothy with his head cocked slightly to the side.

"Well," said the crow, rather precociously, "It's obvious, isn't it? You appear to be heading west, toward the dandelions, when you *could* be heading east, toward the vegetable patch. What's the use expending all that energy for a few dandelion leaves, when you might feast on the carrot tops, peas, green beans and peppers, growing over there? Of course," he added, thoughtfully, "dandelions are alright – I mean, if you like that sort of thing."

"Who are you, please?" inquired Timothy.

"My name is Cornelius," said the crow. "I am a Powhatan corvid. My family has been around these parts for many generations."

"Well, Sir," said Timothy, "How do you do? I would appreciate it if you would kindly let me continue on my way."

"You see," implored the crow, "it's simply the intelligent thing to do."

"What's 'intelligent' exactly?" asked Timothy.

"Well, 'clever'," answered the crow, in a soft voice.

"Then, I don't know," said Timothy, "but it seems to me that my journey on a clear path toward dandelion leaves is quite clever, indeed. And I'm rather hungry, so if you don't mind, terribly, I'll resume my journey now."

Cornelius stretched out a wing and a leg, and then shook his feathers.

"Alright," said the crow, adjusting his position on the perch, "if you think it's best."

Timothy wanted very much to ignore the bird and walk on, but he found he could not do so.

Cornelius kept quizzical, steady eyes focused on the tortoise. He then cleared his throat.

"Ahem. You see, soon there will be others gathering at this veritable banquet. Earlier this morning, I saw Grahame the groundhog making his way through the woods. Grahame and the young groundhogs will demolish the vegetable garden. The dandelions, however, will still be there tomorrow."

"Oh," said Timothy, not quite sure how to respond. And then he added, "You do use very large words, Sir. What's

v-e-r-i-t-a-b-l-e?"

"It's…real," replied the crow.

"Well, you might have said so in the first place," stated Timothy.

Cornelius ignored the remark and preened his feathers to prepare for flight.

"Well," he said at length, "I must be going now. There's a schooner sailing up the York River this morning, and I think I'll hitch a ride."

"Why?" asked Timothy.

"Because, if I sit atop the sails, a seagull will likely drop a fish on the deck for my breakfast, and sailing on a schooner is the most wonderful adventure, with or without breakfast!"

"Cheerio, then," said Timothy.

Cornelius lifted his silken, blue-black wings to the sky, circling the tortoise once before departing.

"Ca-ha, I'll see you later, my little friend," he said.

Timothy waited until Cornelius was out of view. He then turned east and made his way toward the vegetable garden.

Timothy found much more than he expected and was somewhat dazed by the selection. There, in front of him, stood rows of endive, beans, pea pods, radishes, collard greens and other delicacies. Situated nearby, a small stone fountain released a trickle of fresh water into a low basin. The tortoise stood in awe of all that appeared in front of him, but stopped to munch on some fresh clover, as an appetizer; this, too, was a favorite morsel.

Cornelius was now on final approach toward the schooner. He banked his wings to the left and performed a flyover, and then gently settled onto the foresail, landing gear down, at first steadying himself with outstretched wings. The morning breezes delighted his senses as he looked out to the Bay and, beyond it, to the ocean. Down below, the crew was busily occupied with morning duties on deck. Other than a few muted voices and the distant sounds of a mourning dove, Cornelius could hear only the waves softly caressing the schooner's bow and the wind fluttering through the sails. Suddenly, the quiet was disturbed by a flock of ring-billed gulls crossing the river, heading inland toward the farm fields in search of grubs.

The gulls made such a noise that Cornelius, who preferred quiet, had to cover his ears. This, of course, was of little consequence, and the poor crow found himself amid a jarring chorus. The gulls cheerfully presented their morning song:

The gulls dipped their wings in friendship and continued their journey inland, and Cornelius, distracted by the morning chorus, quite forgot the purpose of his journey. Suddenly, breakfast didn't matter very much. Cornelius closed his eyes and relished the fresh Bay air, which sent small ripples through his feathers. He lifted his wings to the sky and glided effortlessly on the warm morning thermals above the schooner. Cornelius thought how very small the humans looked beneath him on the deck!

After a while, he returned to his woodland and saw his new friend, Timothy Trumble, fast asleep in the vegetable

Our Olde Chesapeake Home

Music & Lyrics by
Nuala C. Galbari

The warm Chesapeake Bay
Where Blue Crab and Finfish and Striped Bass play
Where Mussels and Oysters lay rich in the sands
Of our warm Chesapeake Bay

Our olde Chesapeake home
Its Chincoteague beaches where wild ponies roam
The woodlands and marshes and shores of the Bay
By our olde Chesapeake home

In far off lands we may roam
Sailing the islands in waters unknown
Yet schooners that take us away bring us back
To our olde Chesapeake home

Timothy Trumble Meets a Powhatan Corvid

patch. Doubtless, Timothy had eaten rather too much at one sitting and had dozed off among the endive leaves. While Timothy slept, Cornelius remained on the alert for young Miss Tatie, the painted cat, who liked to tease tortoises when she had nothing else to do. Cornelius had little fear of cats. In fact, he had a good sense of humor and he often landed behind the cat and pulled her tail—just for some corvid comedy. Nevertheless, Cornelius kept a watchful eye on Timothy, whose overindulgence in his morning fare had caused him to retreat into his shell for a snooze.

CHAPTER TWO
Grahame Conveys Disquieting News

*A*loud rustling sound came from the woodland. The additional cracking of twigs and branches suggested that an animal of ample size was making its way to the clearing. Cornelius leaned over his perch and surveyed the ground with inquisitive eyes. A rather bulky groundhog burst out from beneath some undergrowth with two young ones in tow. He didn't run, exactly; he tumbled along the ground, his barrel-shaped body pressing significant weight on his short legs.

"Oh, it's you, Grahame!" said Cornelius. "What a commotion you are making!"

"Sorry!" said Grahame, gently. "It's Gareth and Gillian, they're quite animated today."

"Well do keep it down, there's a good chap! I'm trying to catch a midday snooze," said Cornelius, rather crossly.

In order to detract the crow from the pups, Grahame asked, "Have you heard the news?"

"What news?" retorted Cornelius, as though anything important could not possibly have missed his ears.

"About the new development…aaah…between the woodland and the river?" Grahame was almost frightened to utter the words.

Cornelius, who had been half asleep and rather slow to respond, suddenly stood to attention.

"I...I... heard they will clear trees and undergrowth from many acres of our woodland for some human habitat," said Grahame. "I am seeking a new home, as my current residence is close to the edge of the marked area."

"What is marked?" asked Cornelius.

"I saw a line of orange bands and ribbons and..." Grahame's words trailed off to a whisper.

"Then there's nothing else for it," said Cornelius. "We will have to convene a meeting with the council!"

Grahame stood upright on his haunches and waved a paw in agreement. "I'll tell the others," he said.

By the following afternoon, the council had assembled in the clearing, and all members chattered noisily until Cornelius arrived with Octavious, the elder osprey.

Rachel, a somewhat stout raccoon, was chewing nuts in a very noisy manner; however, as soon as Cornelius turned toward her and glanced over his aristocratic beak, she immediately set the nuts down on a nearby log, swallowed rather loudly and then sat up straight with her paws crossed.

A red fox arrived looking harried and quickly took his seat at the edge of the woods. Sebastian the skunk and Obediah the opossum both trundled in somewhat crumpled from sleep and in peevish moods.

Octavious surveyed the group through a monocle and spoke with an authoritative voice, "This meeting is called to order!"

The long, hot, languid mid-summer days had slowed activity in the woodland. Now that the animals had gathered together, there was a joyful clamor, and gradually everyone began exchanging stories about the past winter and spring.

"Too much chatter!" announced Cornelius, with a

solemn expression. We have a potentially grave situation, and we will all need to focus upon a solution."

A small voice in the gathering proclaimed, "But I haven't had any breakfast yet!"

"Silence!" said Octavious. He scanned the group with hunter's eyes. "Now, it is my duty to inform you that the humans have been removing undergrowth in our woodland and tagging trees with orange ribbons. This can mean only one thing: they intend to destroy our homes."

The animals' chatter subsided and the company sat still with all eyes focused on the raptor.

Having now gained the full attention of his subjects, Octavious continued, "While the humans begin moving their machinery into the area, we must stand firm and ready to fight. I have called several of my species from the southern Bay to help, and I appeal to each of you to assemble as many family members and friends as you possibly can to help us confront our foe."

A little voice unexpectedly piped up from behind the group. "What can I do, for I am very small, indeed?"

"Who speaks there?" asked Octavious.

"Please, Sir, it's me, Timothy Trumble," came a gentle reply.

"Well," Timothy Trumble," said the great bird of prey, "You can write pamphlets to assist in our cause. Write among the undergrowth! Write in the sand! Write in the vegetable garden!" Then, stretching his wings, Octavious added, "I charge you with the purpose of carrying the news as far and wide as you can."

"Oh yes, Sir," said Timothy. "Indeed I will gather my chelonian friends and, together, we will send dispatches throughout our colony."

Octavious was well pleased with the optimism of this

very small tortoise, and he looked down upon him with kind eyes.

"Well," said Octavious, "there it is for now! Go forward all, and save our woodland."

CHAPTER THREE
Rupert and the Flight Cadets

Early the next morning, Cornelius flew out to the river. He perched on the highest branch of a red oak tree and looked out toward the Bay. Cornelius needed time alone to clear his head and consider his strategy. He looked down thoughtfully at some gulls that had gathered on the beach below. As he watched the birds, who appeared to be talking in a group, he suddenly recognized the gulls as those who had serenaded him on the schooner the prior morning. Just then, an enterprising ring-billed gull flew up to the red oak and summoned him.

"Hello there!" said the gull, warmly. "We haven't been introduced, but my silly name's Rupert – Squadron Leader Rupert Gull."

"How do you do," said Cornelius.

"Very well, I am sure," replied Rupert. "We have received news of your dilemma," he said. "It is most worrying."

"How did you hear of our troubles?" asked the crow.

"News travels fast on prevailing winds," said the gull. "Anyway, if there is anything we can do, please call upon us!. . ."

A tentative Cornelius interrupted Rupert in mid-sentence. "Indeed, you might be of assistance."

"Well," said Rupert, "some of the flight cadets are not

quite up to the mark yet, however, we can sing – at least we try. I myself am a composer of nautical ballads, you know, 'sea shanties' some call them."

"I am rather particular when it comes to music," said Cornelius, "and not very partial to the harmonica. The singing all seemed rather atonal to me."

"Oh, that!" said Rupert smiling. "I was training the flight cadets in *a capella*. It was their first practice session."

As the two birds conversed, Rupert suddenly let out a loud gasp. "Oh no!" he exclaimed. "Not again!"

"What is the trouble?" asked Cornelius.

"Please excuse me, Cornelius," said Rupert, "I must

attend to the class. It's the cadets – they've taken off to buzz the schooner again! It's a mischievous habit." Rupert lifted off and climbed rapidly, gaining altitude over the gull cadets.

Cornelius could not help but laugh, and he was forced to cover his beak with a wing to hide his amusement. However, while watching Rupert regroup the young offenders, it suddenly occurred to him that the scene had attracted many citizens on the beach. The young gulls' antics had indeed caused quite a commotion. Here was an opportunity, he thought.

At that, Cornelius departed to the west, seeking Octavious and Rachel. During the morning, he had considered how he might save the woodland home and now an idea presented itself quite clearly. Not having eaten any breakfast, he felt a little light-headed and took advantage of the warm thermals rising from the bridge, drifting effortlessly for several minutes. Ahead of him, the gull cadets now flew in a tight formation, with Rupert bringing up the rear guard. Cornelius dipped a wing in Rupert's direction and continued to the woodland.

Cornelius came in for a short landing. Temporarily distracted by Timothy, who was tripping at quite a pace toward the clearing in the wood, he almost collided with a falling walnut tree:

"Look out there, cousin!" shouted a blue jay as Cornelius brushed against a large branch and then collided with some ripe walnuts.

"Are you alright, Uncle?" asked a young crow, earnestly.

Cornelius gathered limb and feather, stood up somewhat shakily, and shook himself off. Suffering from only a slight loss of dignity, he responded,

"Yes, nephew, I am quite alright."

Cornelius suddenly realized that Timothy Trumble had been near the tree when it fell. He called out an immediate search and the blue jays and young fish crows covered much ground before locating Timothy, who was found in upside-down position, beside one of the branches.

"Phew!" said Timothy Trumble, "that was rather too near!" And then he stretched out his neck and, taking hold of a large leaf with his jaws, pulled himself right side up.

As the friends ate supper and talked of their day, the distant strains of the gulls' *a capella* choir drifted across the airwaves and through the Loblolly pines that seemed to sway, lightly, to the music.

"It must be wonderful to fly, Mr. Cornelius, Sir," said Timothy Trumble, presently.

"It is, Timothy," said Cornelius.

"Does the world look very different from up there, Sir?" asked Timothy as he munched on some endive he had brought from the garden.

Cornelius turned to his friend, "When you look down from above, you see the lushness of the forest. You see the inlets flowing into the rivers, the rivers flowing out to the ocean and the ocean gently touching the sands. You see blues and aquamarines and greens – all the colors and patterns of our remarkable planet. When you fly and look down upon our world, everything seems smaller and more fragile. To fly is to feel that fragility and yet to breathe the spirit of life and stroke heaven with your wingtips."

Timothy Trumble stood for a moment in quiet contemplation of these words.

"Oh, Mr. Cornelius, Sir," he said at length, "I am only a small tortoise, but you have shown me something quite different today. Quite different."

The tortoise looked closely at his new friend and considered his bright, intelligent eyes and his smooth silken feathers.

"I wish I were a crow," he said.

It was now quite late, and the raccoons and opossums were just awakening and making quite a clamor while the birds and other animals were trying to sleep.

Cornelius lowered himself on the perch, closed one eye and contemplated a cricket with the other one. Tomorrow he would speak with Octavious, Rupert and the young gulls, but night was upon the woodland. He was safe among friends, and all was now serene.

Just before he settled in, Cornelius felt a presence nearby on an adjacent perch. Looking round, he came beak-to-bill with a great horned owl.

"I've been listening to your conversations," said the owl, rather forwardly, "and I think I may be of help. By the way, my name's Olandra."

But Cornelius was very tired and in no mood for an interfering owl, so he didn't answer.

CHAPTER FOUR
Dispatching the Company

"Now hear this," said Octavious, addressing the raccoons and the opossums, "we must move tonight! There is no time to dally."

The assemblage stood to attention, and all the woodland creatures were quiet, awaiting instructions from the osprey.

"Rachel, you will enlist five raccoons. And Obediah, you will gather your family to assist the raccoons. All must leave the woodland by dusk and travel to the river. Tonight, you will prepare a banner and by dawn, Rupert and the young gulls will help you tie it to the aft mast of the schooner. Tomorrow, when the schooner sails up the river, our banner will fly high and all who see it will read of our plight."

Cornelius then moved to garner the animals' support. "All in agreement, say aye!"

The company all voiced their 'ayes' and the plan was approved.

At dusk, a small band of raccoons and opossums entered an old riverboat, and with Rachel at the helm, journeyed down the inlet to the river, rowing very softly so as not to be heard. Along the creek they rowed, with only a small lantern to guide them. They entered the river and drifted quietly along until the schooner came into sight. The schooner creaked gently in the water, pulling lightly on her ropes as though in a silent endeavor to cast her moorings and sail. As the little boat traveled alongside her hull, Rachel spelled out her name, S-o-l-a-r-i-s, then whispered, "Schooner *Solaris*."

She was a glorious vessel, a gaff-rigged schooner that wintered in the Caribbean islands of Antigua and Barbuda, but spent her summers in the Chesapeake Bay. Sometimes, on special occasions, she sailed up to Maine and joined other tall ships, but the Chesapeake Bay was home to the Solaris and her crew. Each spring, the citizens of the Bay would welcome her home after her winter sojourn in the Caribbean; the animals knew that each time the Solaris sailed the Bay, she attracted much attention.

The raccoons brought the little boat to the port side and the opossums quietly climbed her ropes. When the 'all clear' was given, the raccoons left the rowing boat and joined the opossums. The crew was asleep, and the animals silently made their way below deck to the hold, where they planned to hide until dark. The animals intended to find some material and writing utensils and work, overnight, on their banner, so there would be little rest, as all paws needed to be industrious. Searching around the vessel, they found a large cotton sheet and, slipping into the captain's office, they also found some markers that would prove excellent for lettering.

Unfortunately, as the animals made their way around the vessel, they encountered something they had not expected: a large Siamese cat, named Beauregard. He sniffed them out, and before he could awaken any of the crew, he had to be harnessed in a corner of the hold.

It was past three o'clock in the morning when the animals completed their banner. They held it up at both ends and looked on with pride at their work. It read, "SAVE OUR OLD WICOMICO WOODLAND!"

The animals were now tired and hungry and looked

around for some food. The raccoons and the opossums were quite used to eating through the night, sleeping during the day, and they needed to return to their rowing boat before dawn, so as not to be seen by the crew. In the ship's store by the galley, they found all sorts of wonderful things to eat. There were fruits and vegetables, biscuits and bread, cheese and even cat food, so they placed a few morsels in a dish for Beauregard, and gave him a saucer of warm milk. They ate and ate and ate, until most of the ship's stores were empty. Rachel found a store of peanuts and devoured them all. Having indulged rather too much in the galley supplies, the raccoons and opossums fell into deep sleep and snored so loudly that Beauregard had to cover his ears with his paws.

And so it was that the raccoons and the opossums awakened very late the next morning to find themselves sailing *aboard* the Schooner *Solaris* – not up the river, but to a strange place named Assateague Island.

Octavious soared over the river and found only the little rowing boat, now adrift near the inlet, its oars neatly laid inside the empty boat.

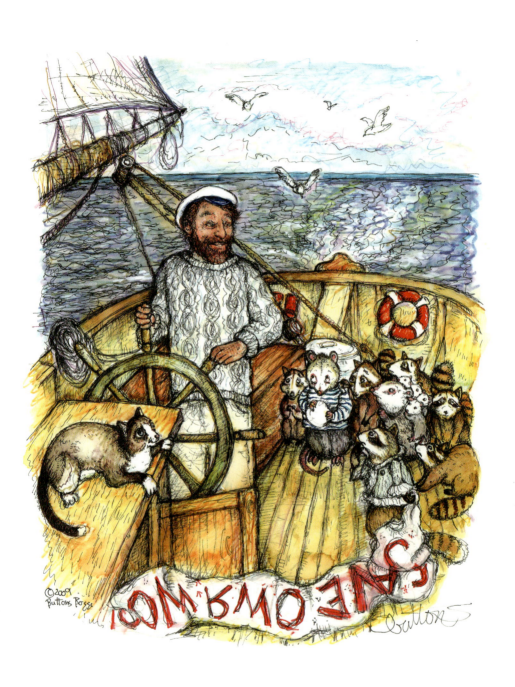

CHAPTER FIVE
Stowaways

The morning was cool and the Bay calm, with soft breezes. Obediah, who had already held a meeting with the opossums to discuss what should be done, had awakened Rachel and the other raccoons. Once the group had agreed to the plan, Obediah would summon the captain and crew and explain their predicament. Looking over to the corner of the hold, Obediah noticed that Beauregard had slipped his harness.

"Isn't that just like a cat?" he said. "Now our troubles will be all the more difficult!"

There was a general y-a-w-n-i-n-g agreement among the animals.

"You must look lively!" said Rachel. "This is no time for sleepiness."

Led by Obediah, the animals proceeded to the deck and lined up in a neat formation, to show respect for their elders.

"Good morning!" said Captain John Farley, rather more kindly than they expected. "I see we have new recruits!"

Beauregard sat close to the captain on the upper deck, narrowed his eyes slyly and smiled intently. Generally bored with the morning activities, Beauregard decided to have a bath.

Obediah cleared his throat and began to explain, but before doing so, he politely removed his hat.

"You see, Sir, our homes are in peril, and we only intended to make a banner to fly from your vessel."

Feeling as though he wasn't quite making sense, Obediah continued, "What I mean, Sir, is that . . . we were rather distracted by the food, for we had not eaten for some time. We meant only to attach the banner and then leave the schooner and row back to our woodland."

All the animals stood to attention, their eyes so hopeful and their expressions so honest that Captain Farley felt a sudden admiration for the group. Rachel, who had been the last to come up on deck, trailed the white banner dejectedly behind her.

The animals maintained a silence, until at length the captain spoke.

"Well," he said with great compassion and kind eyes, "Some of the supplies have been eaten, but there is no harm done. Beauregard has spoken of your kindness and, upon hearing of your troubles, pleaded your case. We will meet later to discuss how we may help you. But first," he said, rather more firmly, "we must sail to Assateague Island, for we have business there. And you, my little friends, must learn some seamanship!"

There was great merriment among the animals, for they had at first considered that they had failed their family and friends. Still, a messenger was needed to take the news back to the woodland. Octavious and Cornelius would be searching for them, and the elders would be apprehensive by the news of their disappearance.

Just then, Rachel spotted a flock of gulls following the schooner. As the gulls neared the vessel, she recognized Rupert and the flight cadets, who had been sent on a search to find the animals.

"Well, young stowaways," said the captain, "send word

with the gulls that all is well, and we will soon return to the river."

The crew, quite accustomed to new recruits, held a class on seamanship, and directed each animal in its duty while on board ship. Rachel, who was very fond of food, was assigned to kitchen duty, where she was also introduced to rationing each crewmember's food supplies, including her own! Obediah was assigned to the upper deck under the tutelage of the first mate.

The next morning, as they sailed the southern Chesapeake Bay, the animals and crew sang a very merry song while they worked on the decks, learning their new trades. They sang in fine form, if not always in perfect tune.

Following a very hard day's work, the animals joined the captain and crew in their quarters and dined on some very fine comestibles. They drank a toast to their new friends. Beauregard dined especially well on a portion of finfish, and there was great merriment and singing throughout the evening.

After some time had passed, Captain Farley asked the animals about their woodland home.

Obediah spoke passionately about his little bunker in the south wood, and how he had spent much time in and around the marina, searching for fish and watching the boats travel up the river.

Rachel told stories of her family and how she and her sisters used to climb the tallest pines when they were still kits, each one trying to climb higher than the others.

"When we were very young, Sir, our woodland supported many species; but for some time now, the humans have been moving closer and many of our families have left for fear of injury or entrapment. We are just a small group of animals now, Sir, but we don't wish to leave our homes."

"Well," said Captain Farley kindly, "if we all put our heads together, I am sure we can find a way to save your woodland."

"It's just that we cannot travel too far, Sir. You see, it's not the distance, but the roads.

"Many of our relatives have died on the roads, Sir. Perhaps the humans don't mean to hurt us, but they don't always see us. We thought about going to see the workmen, but we didn't think they would listen to our story."

Captain Farley smiled. "Don't worry about that now. There may be some who are insensitive to your concerns, but there are those who work very hard to help you, and who understand your fears."

Rachel and Obediah smiled a little nervously, however they felt they could trust Captain Farley.

"Keep a hopeful heart, and all will be well!" said the captain.

There followed a round of songs and everyone joined in the nautical rhymes.

The animals all settled into their bunks, sleepy, happy and optimistic that the next day would bring good fortune in their direction. Sailing in the Schooner *Solaris* was the most excellent adventure. Still, before they slept they thought of their woodland and felt considerably homesick. Soon they were rocked to sleep by the soothing sounds of the Bay waters.

Messing About On Schooners

Music & Lyrics by
Nuala C. Galbari

There are abundant duties when you answer the ocean's call.
You learn the navigational aids and hoisting the sails so tall;
Hauling the halyards, swabbing decks, and cooking for one and all--
Adventure and fun and sea and sun--a life that will enthrall.

Sailing the Caribbean in her waters so clear and blue,
Meeting oceanic friends of every genus and hue;
We can explore the islands as we travel the whole year through.
I can't imagine anything else that I would rather do!

Maybe we'll meet some pirates as we conquer the southern seas.
Perhaps we'll find some hidden treasure buried beneath the trees;
Dancing to island music in the soft Caribbean breeze
And more attendant pleasures as we sail around at ease.

Reprise (Verse 1)

CHAPTER SIX
Arrival of the Apparatus

Octavious and Cornelius returned to the woodland and summoned the animals to a meeting. There was no sign of the schooner on which they believed the raccoons and the opossums had sailed. However, Cornelius had been flying up and down the river where the schooner was last sighted, and he had sent Rupert and the gulls to search the Bay. Cornelius was confident he would soon receive word. As the elder and the chief, Octavious was occupied in another direction: watching the movement of the humans at the edge of the woodland. It was true that the news was not good. The machinery had been brought in, but the large hog brush cutters and forestry tree shears sat idle, like sleeping red dragons.

The word had gone out to all the animals that their homes were in danger. While the other tortoises traveled all around to write messages in the soil and on the narrow riverbank beaches, Timothy took a break from his calligraphy and advised the woodland residents to gather their young ones and listen for the alarm that Olandra, the great horned owl, would signal throughout the forest. But then, the storms crossed the Appalachian Mountains, heavy thunderstorms bearing down on the woodland, flooding the clearing, the woods and the open land. Ground-to-cloud lightning struck two of the woodland's aged trees, and the thunderclaps were so loud that the animals covered their ears, shaking with terror on their pins. The tortoises sought cover in the undergrowth and withdrew into their shells. The corvids sat low in the trees with closed wings and the groundhogs retreated to their warrens. It rained and rained, a long line of storms repeatedly attacking the woodland, until all the messages the tortoises had written were washed away, and the results of several days' hard work were undone. The tortoises were saddened and their hearts were heavy. Timothy Trumble had walked so far and written so much that his legs were very sore indeed.

Finally, the storms traveled out to the Atlantic Ocean and calm was restored. Cornelius flapped his wings sturdily and then stretched them out to dry in the morning sun. While he contemplated the storm damage, his little friend reappeared, and with a voice that was especially cheerful, said,

"Good morning, Mr. Cornelius, Sir. I am up early as I have much work to do restoring my messages on the riverbank beaches."

Cornelius, rather damp and windblown, was enlivened by Timothy Trumble's optimistic voice. He flew down to Timothy Trumble and warmly touched the top of his shell with a wingtip.

"Yes," young Timothy," said the corvid. "You are quite right – we must promptly resume our work. *Tempus fugit!*"

"What is *tempus fugit?*" asked Timothy with a puzzled expression, for the tortoise had no Latin.

"It means, 'time flies'," said Cornelius.

"But what *is* time, exactly, Sir?" queried Timothy.

Cornelius removed his spectacles and looked up to the sky. The strong winds had pushed the storm clouds briskly out to the Atlantic Ocean, revealing a clear azure ceiling.

"Time is…Time is the space in which we work, with love, for others." The crow looked at Timothy Trumble, brushing some leaves off his shell. "Time is…sometimes difficult to explain. It's rather like a journey."

Timothy then said, "How do we know time, Sir?"

"We animals know it by the sun, the moon, the stars and the seasons. Humans had to invent machines to measure it, but still, they often waste time."

"Well then, Sir, this morning in the vegetable patch – I was puttering around and chasing butterflies. Was that wasting time?"

"No, Timothy," said Cornelius, with an amused expression. "Puttering around and playing is a very good thing – so long as we attend to our studies and work first.

Consider the words of Henry van Dyke:

'Be glad of life because it gives you a chance to love and to work and to play and to look up at the stars.'"

"If I try to look up at the stars, Sir, it makes my neck sore," said the tortoise, without considering his words.

"Well then," advised Cornelius, "You should practice more often! The greatest challenges in life bring forth the sweetest rewards."

After some time, Cornelius looked around to find the other animals had gradually emerged from burrow, warren, tree and undergrowth, a posse of soggy feather and fur and dampened spirits.

"All listen now," said Cornelius, kindly. "Rupert and the gulls brought news of the raccoons and the opossums this morning. The animals had an unscheduled banquet in the schooner's galley last night, after which they fell asleep. The silly animals found themselves sailing the Chesapeake this morning and making amends for their mischievous behavior."

The squirrels and groundhogs tried very hard not to smile, but it was difficult to keep straight faces.

Cornelius raised his beak and steadied his glance. "We cannot have disobedience in our ranks," he said very sternly. "If we are to fight those who wish to send us out of our homes, we must stand together."

Having gained the animals' attention, Cornelius continued, "This morning, my flock will examine the west woodland to see if any more machines have arrived, and the tortoises will resume their work on the sands. Squirrels, you must gather food, and groundhogs, clear your tunnels for storing supplies. All youngsters must be moved to the east woodland. We will meet with Octavious before dusk."

So off they all went, to nest, warren and burrow, to woodland east and west. Cornelius gathered his cousins, and without a word, they flew to where the machinery stood. There, at mid-morning, as the corvids settled onto the high perches above, the humans discussed the clearing of brush and the removal of loblolly pines, sassafras, and even the pawpaw, among other native trees in the west wood. Cornelius called in other members of the flock and all corvids waited for the secret signal.

"Now, remember," said Cornelius to the younger corvids, "*Primoris operor haud vulnero!*"

The older cousins nodded in agreement, however the younger corvids looked on with blank stares.

Cornelius sighed, "Study your Latin, chaps!" He reminded them, "*Primoris operor haud vulnero* - First, do no harm! What we must simply do at this time is work to postpone operations."

Suddenly, as Cornelius spoke, the humans walked away from their vehicles. Cornelius gave the signal, a quiet "chheeupp" of his beak.

Three members of the flock lifted off silently and landed near the vehicles. Unseen by the humans, who were marking out the first area to be cut, the corvids skipped and hopped across the road, and then flew up to the open windows. One of the corvids grasped some paper in his beak and returned with it to the trees. The others removed the keys from the machinery; crows like to collect shiny objects. It was well known that Cornelius, being a corvid of some great age, had a large collection of spoons, spectacles, old coins, keys and all manner of shiny things, which he stored in the gutters of an historic schoolhouse roof. Cornelius placed his spectacles on his beak and read the words, "Master Plan, Wicomico Woodland."

"Good work, chaps!" said Cornelius. "Now, we must take the plan to Octavious."

As the humans climbed into the brush hogs they

found that none of the vehicles would start. For while the corvids had searched for the papers and removed keys, young squirrel paws were hard at work dislodging some bolts from the machines. The foreman scratched his head in confusion and the crews sat down to eat their packed lunches. The birds noted that the workmen were quite merry.

Cornelius and the flock staged a flyover, and purely for fun, performed a few barrel rolls before returning to base. Busily employed with his writing on the riverbank below, Timothy Trumble looked up to the sky and shook his head at the corvid antics. He knew it was another example of crows and squirrels working in symbiosis, for the tortoise had observed well that when the squirrels buried nuts for the winter, the corvids would later retrieve and eat them.

CHAPTER SEVEN
Assateague Island

The next morning, in variable ocean waters, the Solaris sailed along the Barrier Islands. Rachel had been up before dawn to prepare breakfast, but found several of the animals still snoozing in their bunks, following the lively diversions of the prior evening.

Rachel rang the ship's bell twice: Ding-ding! Ding-ding! Finally, a few peepers opened, and one or two of the opossums slipped out of their bunks. The raccoons did not stir, and Rachel was obliged to awaken each one.

"Wake up! Wake up!" she called. "We'll be docking at Assateague at nine a.m., and everyone must go ashore."

"Oh, very well," said Obediah, rubbing his eyes. "But please," he implored, "no breakfast this morning… ehm…tums is a bit squiffy!"

"Well then, Obediah," said Rachel, "it's burnt toast for you!"

"Burnt toast…?" he asked.

"It's the old sailor's cure," said the raccoon.

The other animals were soon up on deck, and the captain even gave Obediah instruction at the helm as they neared Assateague Island.

"Remember, Obediah," said Captain Farley, "The keel uses the forward motion of the schooner to generate lift. This counteracts the leeward force of the wind."

Obediah turned his head to the right, then to the left, then to the right again, as he tried to pay attention to Captain Farley and manage the wheel at the same time! It was all rather new to him, and it might not have been so difficult to learn had he not been feeling poorly at the time.

"What is *the beam* of the schooner?" asked Captain Farley.

"The beam is…the beam of the schooner is its…widest point."

"That is correct, Obediah. You have learned many things this morning!"

Rachel observed Obediah from a distance and felt rather sorry for the animal, as he was looking somewhat pale, but then it was difficult to tell since opossums have such white faces anyway! For his part, Captain Farley was trying to keep Obediah busy, so that he would forget about his collywobbles!

All the while, Obediah grumbled about his breakfast of black tea and burnt toast. Nevertheless, he was beginning to get his sea paws, and he grew accustomed to life on the schooner. He was dressed in a sailor's hat, shirt and trousers the captain had given him, and he cut a fine figure at the helm, even if he still felt a little out of sorts.

The animals had never been away from their woodland home, except to the creek near the river. Arriving at Assateague Island, they suddenly became very excited. They all stood to attention on the deck, awaiting the captain's permission to disembark.

The gray clouds drifted out to the Atlantic, and the sun returned. Beauregard stretched out on the top deck and began to wash his face.

"Aren't you going ashore, now?" asked one of the opossums.

"Oh, my goodness, no," replied Beauregard, rather self-importantly. "I never leave the schooner!"

Suddenly, Beauregard looked down below just as the animals burst into song:

Assateague Isle

Music & Lyrics by
Nuala C. Galbari

Beauregard had no musical ear at all. He strongly disliked any music and planned a feline revenge for the misery of having to listen to animal and crew ditties! Once the animals were out of sight, he slipped below deck to the kitchen and rearranged the supplies, while also making off with some cheese. While jumping down from the counter, he knocked over a jug of milk, which smashed into small pieces all over the floor. Beauregard stepped carefully over the milk, then shook his paws, smiled, and disappeared into the captain's cabin for a snooze.

CHAPTER EIGHT
Tarquin

Captain Farley led the small entourage of animals ashore. The winds had calmed, and the morning sun cast a splendid lattice of soft light across the island. A herd of painted ponies grazed contentedly on the grasses around the dune and salt marshes, nibbling on bayberry twigs, rosehips and seaweed. The ponies looked on with interest as the raccoons and opossums approached, and a young filly drew near, raising her head in order to catch the scent of the visitors. She was a fine young animal, a painted brown and white filly with a playful air and a friendly nature. She approached the other animals at a brief canter, her legs going in all directions as though slightly out of control. Then, she lifted a front hoof, flicked her tail, and cantered back to her mother. The raccoons and opossums had never seen a pony before and didn't know quite what to make of her. Feeling there was no threat to her safety, the filly once again ventured toward the animals.

"Hello!" she said, merrily. "My name's Penelope. Where do you come from?"

"We're from the Wicomico Woodland," said Rachel rather proudly.

"Wicomico?" replied Penelope. "I've never heard of *Wicomico*."

"It's a small woodland village, near the York River," said Rachel. "Haven't you ever heard of the Powhatan?"

"No," said the filly. "Well, I only know the island - you see I was born here."

"If you don't mind my asking," said Rachel, "did you come here in large boats?"

The filly thought Rachel's question was very funny and rather strange.

"Large boats?" repeated the filly.

"Well, I mean, we animals sailed here on a schooner," said Rachel, with a perplexed expression. "Did you swim from the mainland?"

"Haven't you heard the legend?" replied the filly. "It is believed that my ancestors swam here from a shipwrecked Spanish galleon that foundered off the island during the early seventeenth century. There's a song about the ship that my mother used to sing to me when I was very small.

La Galga de Andalucía

Music & Lyrics by
Nuala C. Galbari

The Woods of Wicomico

2. Tossed in a storm twelve days or more
Hey, La Galga, Ho, La Galga.
The galleon sank on the Eastern Shore
With a hey and a holly, holly ho!

3. Of her crew and passengers, many survived.
Hey, La Galga, Ho, La Galga.
The horses swam to the Barrier Isles
With a hey and a holly, holly ho!

"Is that true?" asked Obediah.

"Well I don't know," said the filly, "the ship existed, but as for the horses - I *do* know that my great-grandmother said it was just a high tale passed down by the stallions."

"Then how *did* the horses arrive here?" asked Rachel.

"My mother told me it was something to do with fencing laws on the mainland," said the filly. "But I do think that the herd can swim well, although I myself have not left the island yet."

"How far do they swim?" asked Rachel.

"Oh, just across the channel at Chincoteague, when the tide is low," said Penelope, "It's a very short swim. The only thing is, some of the ponies do not return. My mother said that the humans take them to the mainland to train them as riding ponies."

"I hope you can stay on your island," said Obediah with a gentle smile. "We miss our home very much. Home is a special place, even if it's just a small burrow or nest, or a tiny warren."

The animals talked for a while and exchanged stories of their dwellings. After some time had passed, Obediah and Rachel called the other animals, many of whom had been puttering around the seashore, and told them it was time to return to the schooner. The captain had said they must be back by one o'clock, and Rachel, looking at the sun's position in the sky, felt it must be nearly time. The animals said goodbye to Penelope and to a friendly piping plover with whom they had held a long conversation at the seashore. A small green treefrog, who was taking an afternoon nap, waved goodbye. As they neared the schooner, they saw a young boy standing on the main deck.

Tarquin, the captain's son, had been visiting an aunt for a few days. His aunt had taken him around the island

and told him of the many different species of bird, fish, mammal, reptile and amphibian on Assateague. Tarquin loved animals, and he very much wanted a painted pony. His aunt said he might choose one at the pony swim to Chincoteague.

Tarquin left the schooner to greet his father, who arrived with two new members of the Solaris crew. Captain Farley had called the animals to the schooner as he planned to depart for Chincoteague, the southern end of the island, at three o'clock.

While the opossums and the raccoons had been visiting with the ponies and discovering the northern seashore, Captain Farley and Tarquin had prepared a surprise for the animals. As they arranged for departure, Tarquin gathered the animals together on deck.

"Tomorrow morning," said Tarquin excitedly, "we will attend the pony swim! You are all invited!"

There was a chorus of "hurrahs" and many happy faces all around!

The animals boarded the Solaris and resumed their work on deck. Obediah checked the schooner's equipment, and the other opossums took their positions on deck to prepare for departure. Rachel went below to check all the galley supplies and equipment and to ensure there was enough food for the journey. As she entered the galley, Rachel said hello to Beauregard, who appeared to be just passing through. Beauregard gave her a rather defiant look as he slinked toward the crew's quarters, pausing for a moment to wash. Rachel wasn't quite sure if Beauregard was washing his face, or if he was washing his paws and wiping them on his face. She studied the cat and thought upon this puzzle for a few moments before beginning her work. She felt instinctively that Beauregard was planning something mischievous, in the way that cats do. Looking around the galley, Rachel didn't notice anything was amiss; the ship's cook had cleaned up the milk that Beauregard had spilled earlier. Rachel therefore settled into her bunk to take a short nap before commencing dinner preparations.

It was a glorious evening. The sun descended slowly into the horizon, sending ripples of warm, orange light across the ocean. Small white caps danced nimbly on the water, and the schooner heeled slightly to the leeward side, her sails billowed by light winds. Rachel and Obediah climbed to the upper deck and looked out to the ocean. They stood in silence, listening to the wisdom of the winds and the calls of the gulls near shore. They thought how immense the ocean, and how small and unimportant their woods must be to humans. Perhaps, after all, nothing could be done and they would just have to accept that their homes would be destroyed. Their home suddenly seemed so far away, and at dusk, with all the excitement of the day behind them, they felt rather sad.

Still, Rachel was learning to be a better cook, and Obediah was learning seamanship well beyond that of rowing a small boat up the creek, although this, too, required a certain skill.

The ship's cook served some very fine food at dinner, and the captain complimented Rachel for assisting the cook so well. He also praised Obediah for his proficiency at the ship's wheel. Captain Farley observed that when Obediah was off-duty, he often had his snout buried in a book on seamanship, a volume that one of the crew had given him. After dinner, Tarquin brought a long muslin bag into the galley. He gave the large object to Rachel and Obediah.

"This is a present from my father and me. I hope you will like it," said Tarquin.

When the animals opened the bag, they found a

striking banner, carefully prepared in fine calligraphy on canvas. The large banner read:

Chesapeake Bay Animals and Friends
Working Together to Save our Woodland

The raccoons and opossums shed some tears of joy, and all gathered to enjoy some music and dance. Tomorrow they would see the ponies and then sail south toward their home.

While the crew and the animals slept, Beauregard worked methodically in the galley, tearing open bags of grain, knocking over containers of sugar, porridge, coffee, tea, milk, jam and anything else he could get his teeth or paws into. When he had finished, the galley floor looked like an artist's palette. Beauregard then slipped into his cat basket, stretched out two front paws innocently, and fell asleep.

CHAPTER NINE
Penelope

The next morning, Captain Farley, Tarquin and the animals set out for the pony swim. The morning had begun calmly, yet Captain Farley had told the crew that the shipping forecast was not very good, and he watched as clouds of deepening gray began to form in the far west. There was barely a whisper of wind when they crossed the island, and the stillness and humidity seemed to portend inclement weather.

Rachel had spent much of the early morning repairing the damage Beauregard had caused. The cat had vanished and did not show up for breakfast. It occurred to Rachel that Beauregard was perhaps feeling left out, since the animals had joined the crew for the voyage. Captain Farley and Tarquin would normally have paid him more attention, but for their visitors on board. Rachel considered that she and Obediah might include Beauregard in their daily duties and even show appreciation of his feline skills. After all, although the cat didn't do much on board, he did discourage mice and rats from entering the schooner at the harbors, and he normally joined the night watch when other members of the crew were asleep at port. If anything was awry, Beauregard would know immediately.

There were thousands of people gathered for the pony swim, and the mood was one of great anticipation.

Penelope

The animals watched eagerly as the ponies and foals swam across the channel to Chincoteague under the watchful eyes of the saltwater riders, who guided their short journey. After the swim, Captain Farley brought Tarquin over to the auction pens to look at some of the foals. As Tarquin looked at the young ponies, he felt that the animal would choose *him*, and he was very happy to know that his aunt would take care of the pony for him and it could still live on the island.

The animals were enthralled by all the ponies' colors and patterns: white, bay, brown, black and white, brown and white, and every shade in between. They thought what a difficult decision Tarquin must have to choose just one, but they knew that he would find the right pony. Suddenly, the animals heard whinnying from a pen, and looked over to see a painted pony looking in their direction. As they approached the pen with Tarquin, they recognized the voice of Penelope.

"Penelope!" Rachel, Obediah and the animals all descended upon the area with greetings and cheering waves.

"I'm frightened," said Penelope. "This morning I was with my mother during the swim, but I don't know where she is now. Why am I in this pen?"

The animals all moved to calm the filly and said that their new friend, Tarquin, was seeking a pony of his own.

"Don't be afraid, Penelope!" said Rachel. "Perhaps Tarquin will adopt you! He's a very kind boy, and his aunt lives on Assateague, so you could still live there."

Tarquin came close to the filly. He stroked her gently on her neck and admired her brown and white painted markings.

"This is our friend, Tarquin," said Obediah.

Penelope nuzzled Tarquin gently and it was obvious

that she and the boy liked each other. The animals held their breath!

"Father, what do you think of her?" asked Tarquin.

"Well, she looks healthy to me. I'll just have one of the crew look at her; her father breeds horses."

The young woman ran her hand down Penelope's legs, fetlocks and hooves to feel for any abnormalities and looked in the filly's mouth.

"Well, she looks good to me."

Penelope kept her eyes fixed on Tarquin. The boy had brown eyes, blond hair that reached his shoulders, and a very amiable face. His hands were gentle and he had a soft voice. Penelope looked at the animals, who stood quietly, not wishing to interfere.

"Do you like her, Tarquin?" asked Captain Farley.

"Yes, Father, I think we will be very good friends. She has spirit but is also gentle."

"Well, then, we'll arrange for her to be taken to your aunt's farm. She can share the stable with the two quarter horses and the new foal."

Tarquin gave his father a hug, and then hugged the pony.

"You'll be home again, soon," he said to the filly.

Everyone was hungry, and they returned to the schooner for some afternoon refreshment. The sun had retreated behind some gray clouds, and there was a distinct scent of rain in the air. The Solaris creaked and groaned in her moorings, as though unsettled, but the animals set to work, and Rachel went below deck with the cook, who had agreed to let her prepare a mid-afternoon surprise for the crew.

Beauregard, having been left alone for the morning with only two crewmembers, had been somewhat impish again. He had chewed the cords of some of the animals' bunks, and had shed quite a lot of fur on Rachel's bunk, where he had been climbing during the morning. He left a small mouse on Obediah's bunk as a welcome back present.

Rachel asked the cook if she might prepare an old recipe, one that was handed down to her from her great-great-great grandmother.

"We'll have to see if we have the ingredients!" said the cook. "What do you need and I'll look in the stores?"

"Well," said Rachel, furrowing her brow, for she had to try and remember the exact recipe, "I'll need, eh… treacle, flour, sugar, cinnamon, butter, salt, spice and milk."

"What's treacle?" asked the cook.

"Oh, it's molasses," said Rachel. "My great-great-great grandmother lived in the woods near a Scottish family. They sometimes gave her treacle scones. One afternoon, she went up to their porch, placed her paws on their window and knocked politely."

"What happened then?"

"Well, my great-great-great grandmother very courteously asked if she might have the recipe."

The cook laughed. "I'm not sure if we have any molasses, but I'll look in the dry stores."

The cook opened a cupboard toward the back of the dry stores and there, indeed, behind the jams, stood a jar of molasses!

"The galley is yours!" said the cook. "I think we have everything else you need."

Rachel put on a white apron, mixed the dry ingredients, poured in the molasses and the milk, and then kneaded the dough. After about five minutes, the delectable scent of the scones wafted from the oven to the upper decks, and made everyone quite hungry. Soon, the crewmembers appeared in the galley to try Rachel's treacle scones.

Captain Farley, speaking with some crumbs on his face, said, "I think we'll employ Rachel as sous chef!"

It wasn't long before the batch of scones had completely vanished!

The crew and the animals returned to their duties on deck. While Rachel was cleaning the kitchen, Beauregard reappeared at the door. Rachel had prepared a special dish of mackerel for the cat. She set the dish down on the galley floor.

"I don't like mackerel," said Beauregard, rather snootily. "It tends to stick in my teeth – thank you all the same."

Beauregard, who if the truth be told really *loved* mackerel, obstinately walked out of the galley and returned to his basket. He knew full well that he was being stubborn. After a short time, Beauregard found he could no longer ignore the call of the fish. He returned to the galley and found the saucer still on the floor. As no one was around to see him, he gobbled up the contents.

The Solaris would depart at dawn for her sail southward. As the crew settled in for the night, Tarquin, who was too excited to sleep, thought about his new pony. Tomorrow, Penelope would frolic in the large paddock at his aunt's farm.

CHAPTER TEN
Mustering the Muskrats

Mukki the muskrat was still up at dawn the next day. He had instructed his family to build additional lodges of cattail and mud along the riverbank to act as lookout posts for the return of the raccoons and the opossums. The lodges were also observation posts for the human activity in the woodland.

Grahame the groundhog had sent two of the youngsters to discuss the building of a new lookout at the edge of the woodland, but the muskrats were busy repairing storm damage to their own homes or rebuilding lodges that had been swept away. The muskrats were about to slip into their burrows to sleep when the groundhogs arrived, so they were a little bit grumpy and very, very tired.

Mukki came to the lodge to speak with the young groundhogs, and, knowing they were chatterboxes, he was careful to bring his talking stick with him.

"Now," said Mukki, calmly, "Could you explain that again, and this time, it would help if only *one* of you spoke!"

The youngsters both started babbling at the same time, one trying very hard to outdo the other one. They made such a noise that no words could be discerned through the jabber.

"Just as I thought!" said Mukki, rolling his eyes. "In that case, we *will* use the talking stick!"

"What's that?" asked one of the groundhogs.

"Have you been skipping class, again?" inquired Mukki. "Our ancestors invented the talking stick for use at tribe council meetings. When our chief is speaking, it is well not to interrupt him, but if you wish to speak, you must wait until the talking stick is passed to you. In this way," Mukki continued, "the talking stick is a courtesy symbol, for it teaches us not only to wait our turn when we wish to speak, but also to listen."

"What is courtesy?" asked the youngest groundhog.

"Courtesy means consideration," said Mukki. "When you are courteous, you consider the feelings and wishes of others.

"Now, you may have the talking stick and tell me what you wish to say. Your friend will refrain from talking."

Mukki raised his eyebrows and looked at the other groundhog.

"*You* will not speak until the talking stick has been passed to you. In this way, we will all take our turn!"

The animal with the talking stick asked, "Why is the stick decorated with feathers, Mr. Mukki?"

"Well, that is to show the significance of the object. Eagle feathers are symbolic and are used for decoration."

The groundhogs looked at each other rather blankly. They didn't really see why a talking stick was necessary at all, let alone why it needed to be decorated with feathers.

Then the second animal said, "Wouldn't it be better to leave the feathers on the eagle in the first place, Mr. Mukki?"

Mukki shook his head and rolled his eyes. "I believe we have wandered from the point of your visit. How can I be of help to you?"

"You see, Mr. Mukki," the first groundhog began, while

firmly holding the talking stick, "Mr. Grahame has asked us to request the building of a new lodge at the southwest creek, so that the muskrats can observe the humans more closely and report back on their activities."

"Yes," said Mukki. "Go on."

The second groundhog took the stick, "Well, it's just that the crows are performing day duty, but we need help with the night watch!"

The young groundhog then passed the talking stick back to Mukki.

"Here you are, Sir," he said, rather precociously. "You can talk now, Sir."

"Well, I will speak with the other animals about your request."

As the groundhogs scuttled away from the lodge, they turned to look back at Mukki from a safe distance.

"*Swamp bunnies!*" they muttered, quietly.

Mukki went down to the creek to munch on some aquatic vegetation while he considered the best position for the new lodge.

Cornelius had been busy helping a fledgling corvid, a young nephew, with his pre-flight lessons. The young crow was born a little late in the season and had a slightly wobbly leg. Although he had been exercising his wings several times a day, his gammy leg prevented him from standing for long, and he frequently flipped over sideways. His parents were out fishing, so Cornelius had taken up the duties of uncle.

Later that morning, while returning from the river toward his nephew's nest with some fish for the youngster, Cornelius heard a strange sound emanating from a large hollow in the ancient red oak tree. Cornelius landed softly on a high branch and stepped sideways to take a closer look. There in the hollow, he saw two peregrine falcon chicks calling for their parents!

Without a word to the young falcons, Cornelius lifted off and flew to the woodland clearing, where Octavious was holding counsel with a number of the adult groundhogs. Grahame looked up just as Cornelius came in for a smooth landing.

Octavious removed his monacle, cleared his throat, and said, "Good afternoon, Cornelius! Do you bring news?"

When Cornelius began to speak, a rather annoying mosquito landed between his eyes, causing the crow to lift his claw and scratch his head, then run to the left, to the right, and finally around in circles.

The mosquito persisted, and every attempt by Cornelius to rid himself of the annoying creature failed.

"Ahem!" said Octavious, as the osprey and the groundhogs stood quite still, patiently awaiting the news.

Although Cornelius wished to give Octavious the report, the crow began hopping around as though his claws were on fire, trying to escape the menacing insect.

"Are you quite all right, Cornelius?" asked the osprey.

Cornelius finally collected himself. "I…bring news of some new residents in the woodland."

The osprey furrowed his brow, and replied, "Well, we certainly need all claws and paws at the ready!"

"No, Sir!" said Cornelius, rather more directly this time. "I mean…*new residents* that may indeed be of critical help in our plight."

At that, Octavious lifted his head and steadied his gaze. The groundhogs pressed their paws together in anticipation.

"I bring news of the peregrine falcon. There is a nesting pair with two chicks in the venerable red oak!"

There were sudden gasps of delight from the groundhogs.

"Peregrine falcons," they intoned, "…in…in…*our* woodland?"

Octavious, responding with notable delight, said, "Call the council for a meeting tonight at six o'clock."

Meanwhile, the muskrats worked steadily to build a new lodge and sent word to all their families to help with supplies.

Not far from the new Muskrat Lodge, the groundhogs methodically carried out their plan to clear several forty-five foot tunnels beneath the humans' machinery. To accelerate their work, the groundhogs pulled miniature carts back and forth on rails, and it was not long before they had completed their task. When they reappeared above ground, their little coats were covered in loam, so they were quite a mess!

It was now time for the animals to reconvene. The cadet gulls had brought word that the *Solaris* was on her way back to the Chesapeake, but Octavious looked to the sky and feared that a storm was brewing in the Atlantic.

The council met at six o'clock sharp. The groundhogs, squirrels, muskrats, tortoises and owls were all in attendance.

"Where are the cadet gulls?" asked Octavious.

"Please, Sir," said Timothy Trumble, "I saw Mr. Rupert with the class just a short time ago. They must be quite near, I think, Sir."

Suddenly, a cacophony of atonal voices was heard at the edge of the woodland.

"Oh no, not again!" said Cornelius, covering his ears, "Here they come!"

Squadron Leader Rupert Gull suddenly flashed past the clearing with a group of young cadets in tow. One of the cadets was out of line, and all the young gulls were heading directly for the edge of the woodland.

"Cedric – your airspeed is too high!" shouted Rupert as Cedric cadet came in for final approach. "Reduce speed! Full flaps!" But it was too late! Cedric smashed into the new Muskrat Lodge, demolishing the lookout post and losing several of his wing feathers at the same time. Poor Cedric landed upside down on the water! When the gull recovered wings, feet, and feather, his eyes met the stares of several rather cross muskrats.

"Ehm…I say, Sir, would this be Muskrat Lodge, by any chance?" asked Cedric.

"It *used* to be!" answered a chorus of muskrats.

Rupert and the flight cadets landed on the riverbank. Rupert approached Cedric, who was now sitting upright in the water, floating nonchalantly near the inlet.

"Well, Sir, I think that went *quite* well…a…a…apart from the loss of a few feathers, that is! A bit of an updraft on final approach there, Sir, but nothing I couldn't handle."

The meeting was called to order. Cornelius reported on the status of the machinery, which was now firmly entrenched in the ground at the edge of the woodland. Timothy Trumble reported that the chelonians had completed their calligraphy on the sands and around the edge of the woods. The tortoises had also carved some messages on the larger tree trunks near the ground, communications that would not be washed away in a storm. The corvids had removed the orange ribbons from the trees, and the muskrats reported that all lodges were repaired, excepting the one that Cedric had just demolished.

Octavious stood silently listening to the reports and then spoke softly. "Tomorrow, the *Solaris* will enter the Chesapeake Bay under full sail, and the gulls report that our banner will fly high for all to see as she sails toward the York River. The word will travel far and wide, and our woodland melee will be known to all!"

The animals all listened intently and with great respect to the noble raptor.

"Now, you have heard that the peregrine falcons have settled in our woodland. All must afford them a warm welcome, and their chicks must be protected. I have made up a duty roster for the corvids and the owls. Cornelius will supervise the day shift, and Olandra will oversee the night shift."

Removing his monacle, Octavious continued, "The great red oak is in the center of the woodland, so we have no need to be concerned at this time that any harm will come to the tree, or the chicks, but we must maintain a constant vigil!"

Then, turning to Squadron Leader Rupert Gull, Octavious said, "Your duty is to patrol the Bay tomorrow, and to observe and report back on the schooner's progress."

Rupert then spoke, "Sir, with your permission, we must return to our base now, for we cannot fly in the dark!"

Octavious bid farewell to the gulls. He was well pleased with the efforts of all the woodland and Bay residents, and it was duly noted in the meeting minutes that the poor muskrats had to put in a little extra time rebuilding the demolished outpost.

CHAPTER ELEVEN
The Sub-Tropical Tempest

The next morning, a gloomy Monday, the humans returned to their machinery. New keys had been acquired for the sleeping dragons, and the nuts and bolts had been replaced.

The crows and squirrels had been up since first light, and they watched the humans through binoculars, from the high trees. One by one, the humans began moving the brush cutters toward the woodland. One by one, the machines sank slowly into the tunnels the groundhogs had cleared on the prior night. When the humans tried to reverse the brush cutters, the ground once again collapsed behind them, until the machines were completely paralyzed. High above the humans, the crows and seagulls danced in the air in a lively manner. Octavious would no doubt be pleased, but the elder osprey was snoozing on his home perch, and no one had the nerve to awaken him during his naps.

At Muskrat Lodge, the young animals swam upstream in the river and kept watch from the old lookouts. The new lodge was undergoing repair after the unfortunate air strike by the cadet gull, who had been grounded for insubordination. This was just as well, because Cedric had lost a number of his flight control feathers and would have to grow them back before he returned to duty. Cedric, who had been assigned to serving breakfast in the officers' mess, was quite put out. However, the

The Sub-Tropical Tempest

cadet gulls had promised they would keep him informed of flight detail, and that morning they were sent out on some navigational duty to track the course of the *Solaris*.

Squadron Leader Rupert Gull and the cadets set out at ten o'clock in a northeast direction. After a while they spotted the *Solaris* sailing around the tip of the Delmarva peninsula. Although she was under full sail, the schooner was making slow progress as the wind velocity increased and the seas became unsettled. The southerly headwinds felt like sandblasts against the gulls' faces.

Looking sideways at a cadet gull, Squadron Leader Rupert Gull said, "It's fortunate that the muskrats did not sail on this voyage! Muskrats are a traditional dish on the Delmarva peninsula. Mukki and the young muskrats are safer in the wetlands near the woods."

"Except, Sir, for the coyote," noted the cadet.

"Hmmm…well, the muskrats do have an advantage over the coyote; they can swim underwater for almost fifteen minutes!"

Rupert looked down below to the deck of the *Solaris* and was greeted by gesturing hands and paws.

Tarquin, Obediah and Rachel waved to the gulls from the upper deck, and the gulls dipped wings in return to say hello. They, too, were having difficulty flying against the prevailing south winds, and the gulls remained close to the schooner as she rounded the peninsula.

On the deck, the animals prepared for tempestuous seas and worked to batten down the hatches to prevent water from entering the hold. Obediah sent the opossums to reef the topsails, while the captain explained the navigational charts to Tarquin. Climbing the ropes with two crewmembers, the opossums suddenly felt a little light-headed.

"It's not quite the same as looking down from a tree in the woodland, Sir," a rather shaky opossum said to one of the crew.

"I mean, I am really good at climbing, but there is usually solid ground beneath me!"

"Don't look down! Don't look down!" shouted the crewmember above him. "Keep your gaze upward, and attend to your duties."

Half way up the mizzen, a younger opossum gripped the mast firmly. He was laughing so much, he thought he might lose his hold!

As he climbed the mast, the younger animal gazed around in awe of the sight before him. Looking leeward toward the Atlantic Ocean, he could see bottlenosed dolphins swimming near the schooner. The school of dolphins swam in almost a parallel line with the *Solaris*, flying through the air at one moment and diving at the next. As they jumped playfully out of the water, they smiled at the animals and sang, *"All is well! We are your escorts!"* The liveliness of the dolphins was a cheering sight, and the young opossum proceeded up the mizzen with great enthusiasm. While his shipmate clung desperately to the forward mast, the young opossum looked out to sea, enthralled by the vast ocean before him, for he had never seen a thing of such beauty before. Above them, Rupert and the cadet gulls flew in a tight formation, ever watchful.

On the captain's order, Obediah turned the wheel of the *Solaris* to the west, and they began their journey across the Chesapeake Bay and then north toward the York River. The thought that they were now journeying home suddenly brought tears to their eyes. Obediah began to sing, and the young opossums and raccoons, together with a chorus of cadet gulls, sang a simple melody that touched the hearts of the captain and the crew.

Sailing Home

    3. Calling us home.
We're going home
Sailing down the creek
To our Powhatan home.
Sailing far away
In the waters blue
Meeting new acquaintances
Yet missing friends we knew.

    It seemed to be a rather sad song, yet when the animals had sung the last line, they were filled with good spirits and merrily went about their duties with the renewed vigor one feels when on the return journey.

    As Captain Farley looked out to the Atlantic, a volatile

weather pattern emerged. Obediah, now dressed in a waterproof Macintosh and hat, took the helm from the first mate and found it more difficult to steer the schooner. As the wind speed increased to forty knots, the raccoons stood watch, and the opossums inspected the halyards and the sails. The *Solaris* keeled heavily to the leeward, and Obediah thought this must be the most exciting day he had ever encountered, although he was not without some fear. The winds increased, and cumulonimbus clouds loomed closer to the Bay. Obediah thought of the early schooners that brought sugar and spices from the West Indies to the New World, and how dangerous the lives of pirates must have been! He rather liked the life at sea! Captain Farley called the crew and animals stationed amidships and advised that a pin on the foresail had snapped and would have to be replaced. A small section of the mainsail had also ripped and would require repair when they returned to the marina.

Suddenly, as the *Solaris* lurched hard to the leeward, Rachel, who had just appeared on deck, caught sight of Beauregard. The cat had been washed sideways in a wave and was sliding toward the bulkhead. With spiked fur, enlarged pupils and claws fully extended, Beauregard slid backwards, choked with fear, desperately trying to hold fast to the pine. Rachel staggered to the left and to the right in an earnest effort to stay upright and help Beauregard. Another wave washed the decks, and both Rachel and the cat slid together toward the bulkhead, holding each other tightly. While the schooner leaned to the windward, Rachel managed to pull Beauregard below deck to the captain's quarters, drying him off with one of the captain's towels. The cat was out of breath and coughed, spluttered and squeaked, until finally he licked his lips and raised his ears. Then Beauregard stood up shakily and pressed his head and purred against Rachel's arm. Rachel, who was also quite out of breath, stroked the cat warmly, but couldn't help thinking how amusing he looked with wet, spiked fur and a rat-like tail!

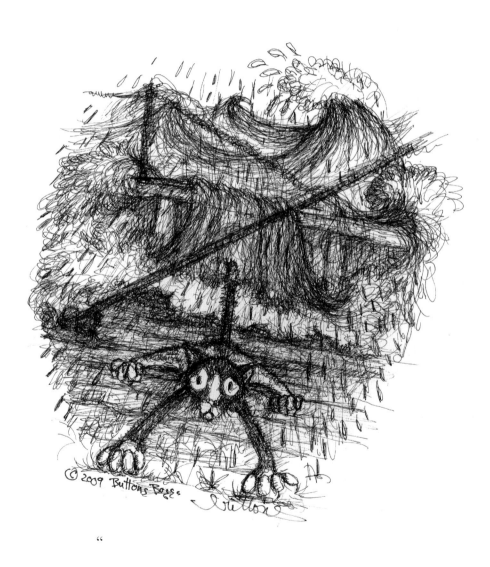

"

Oh, thank you Miss Rachel, indeed I thank you!" said Beauregard. He then began to wash, but sneezed suddenly, as his fur was rather salty.

"Perhaps I need to rinse your coat with warm water," said Rachel.

As the animals spoke, the schooner swayed again, and Rachel and Beauregard went together to the ship's galley to heat a little water on the cast iron stove.

After his coat had dried, Beauregard climbed into his basket, although he was still rather shaken, and Rachel began dinner preparations, even though she didn't think anyone would be very hungry. Beauregard looked up at his new friend, smiled at her, and then tucked his nose under his paws and closed his eyes. Obediah had just come off duty. He was very tired, as it was difficult trying to keep the schooner on course during the high winds. He had some tea and a sandwich in the galley before going to sleep. The first mate had taken the wheel, and Captain Farley came to the galley to report that the winds had changed direction, and the wind speed had dropped to thirty knots as they sailed northwest towards the York. Still, Rachel and her pots and pans were sliding back and forth in the galley, and she thought about her woodland burrow and how she looked forward to a long, calm sleep when she returned.

Up on deck, one of the crew instructed the opossums on making a monkey's fist knot around a small weight to use as a heaving line.

The opossums were quite excited about the monkey's fist and thought that this knot-on-a-rope would be useful in their woodland, especially for use in knocking fruit and nuts down from the trees!

When the opossums had mastered the skill (even though their particular monkey's fists were very small), they all shouted, "Huzzah!"

They practiced and practiced, until they had a barrel full of the knots!

As the *Solaris* sailed to the mouth of the York and the wind speed settled to a comfortable fifteen knots, everyone began to smile again, and finally, their appetites returned. The dark clouds passed and at length the sun peeped through and twinkled on the waves.

While the schooner entered the York River, and the opossums, the raccoons and the crew stood in a neat line on deck, the ship's sails billowed gently in the soft winds, and the banner flew high from the mizzen mast so that all those gathered on shore could read her message:

Chesapeake Bay Animals and Friends
Working Together to Save our Woodland

As the crowd watched from shore, the *Solaris* sailed into Yorktown. Rupert and the flight cadets performed an aerobatic feat around the schooner, and the crowds cheered and waved. The gulls then performed a joyful medley of songs. Even Beauregard reappeared on deck, quite dry by now and wearing a blue hat in honor of the Air Force!

CHAPTER TWELVE
Sebastian

The *Solaris* slowly made her way up the York River at dawn under half sails. Captain Farley put in at a small marina close to the woodland. There, the *Solaris* would spend the next week, and the crew would repair the damage. The raccoons and opossums had lost their land legs, and although they were overexcited by the thought of seeing their home again, they disembarked on shaky pins and zigzagged giddily on the little dock.

Then, in a heartfelt show of love for the edge of their woodland, (or perhaps still in a state of dizziness), the animals all fell, facedown, on the sandy shore, giggling with sheer excitement at the thought of being home again.

Timothy emerged from the undergrowth, rubbed his eyes, and followed a narrow path to the clearing in the wood. The squirrels and groundhogs had been up since dawn, having received word that the *Solaris* would soon return. Although most of the animals had moved their quarters toward the east woodland, Cornelius and the young corvids had brought news that the humans were busily employed trying to remove the machines from the ditches into which they had slumped. No work had begun in the woods, and several of the 'for sale' signs seemed to have disappeared, overnight, from the north section. As the corvids watched the humans that morning, there seemed to be some disagreement about boundary lines, and a ravine running through the center of the woodland was apparently deeper and longer than the humans had anticipated.

Octavious took his position in the clearing and looked down upon the gathered crowd.

"Now, I will tell you this," he said, pausing for a moment to quiet the animals, "our work in this matter has been of vital importance. The humans have not made any progress, their machines are not operating at present, and there have been other delays, due to the nature of the woodland and its ravines." Octavious then continued, "While our woodland is as yet undisturbed, we must continue our efforts to ensure we remain vigilant. The gulls bring word that the raccoons and opossums will soon be home. They have fulfilled their duties, and many other species have read the banner flying over the Bay and the river."

Cornelius then spoke, "Be calm and carry on with your normal duties today, play with your young, but stay in the east woodland until we have further news...." Cornelius then broke off, and the animals all became rather quiet as an unusual sound began emanating from the north woods. It was not a sound with which they were familiar. Timothy Trumble looked up at Cornelius and said, "Would you like me to go and discover the cause of the noise, Sir?"

Cornelius smiled, "Dearest Timothy, you have a good heart, but I think that might be a slower way of identifying the source, and I wouldn't wish you to be in any danger. Allow the corvids to approach the area first."

"Very well, Sir," said Timothy, not at all dismayed by the response, and the little tortoise turned in the direction of the sound and began a slow, steady walk. Several of the corvids flew in the same direction, but they could not detect the reason for the tap-tap-tapping noise that reverberated throughout the woodland. Wary of snakes, the corvids did not wish to land in the brushwood.

Cornelius flew from one tree to the next, and to the next, keeping his eyes on Timothy Trumble.

"Mr. Cornelius," said Timothy at length, "It's just that…well, it's not always necessary to be fast, is it, Sir?"

"What is your meaning?"

"Well, Sir, it seems to me at least…everything that moves slowly…eh…lives longer! I am a slow thing in a fast world, but I think that's quite alright, really," said the little chelonian. Cornelius was about to interrupt the tortoise, but then Timothy Trumble continued.

"You see, Sir, take, for example, the sea turtle…I mean, the sea turtle lives a long time, over 100 years. And then there's the elephant, well that's about seventy years, and the manatee, up to sixty years. Then, the giant tortoises of the Galapagos Islands, they can live to 150 years, I think. They are all long-lived species as far as I know, Sir. Oh, and the crocodile…yes, definitely the crocodile, that would be about seventy years, and…."

Cornelius felt that he had to interrupt the chatterbox. "Yes," he said, "They are all long-lived species."

The crow smiled, as he found he could not dispute Timothy Trumble's claim.

"Each one of us has his or her own natural pace," said Cornelius. "It is good to find that pace and live in this manner."

Timothy followed a winding path through the undergrowth, pushing aside twigs and Virginia creeper as he made his way toward the inlet. The tap-tap-tapping became louder, and eventually Timothy could see black and white fur extending from behind a large log.

"Who goes there?" asked a rather petulant voice, the animal raising his tail high in the air.

"It's Timothy Trumble," came the reply.

"Are you the tortoise?"

"Yes, Sir, I am. We could hear the tapping from the east woodland. We wondered…."

The voice interrupted. "You may approach, but don't step on my material!" The animal lowered his tail.

As Timothy made his way around the end of the log, he saw Sebastian the skunk tapping steadily on his sewing machine. The skunk had cleared some brush in a small area around the trunk of a sweetgum tree and had set up his little sewing area near the base of his burrow.

Sebastian was a rather solitary animal, and he usually worked on his own, preferring to be self-sufficient. While he sometimes made clothing for the animals, he kept to himself much of the time, but it seemed to Timothy Trumble that he was really very kind underneath his grumpy exterior and that he might welcome some company, if it was given.

"Would you like some tea?" asked Sebastian. "There's still some freshly brewed in the pot, if you would care to help yourself. It's Oolong – if that's not too smoky for your taste."

Timothy Trumble poured himself a very small cup, although he didn't like Oolong tea at all! Still, he wished to appear gracious.

"What is it you are making?" asked Timothy, after sipping the tea.

"Parasols!" said Sebastian, without any further explanation.

"Oh, to provide shade in the clearing, I suppose?" ventured the tortoise.

"No! No! Not at all!" said Sebastian.

Timothy quickly realized that perhaps Sebastian was simply not used to conversing with others, as he spent many days alone and had no immediate family members in the woodland. The tortoise tried another approach.

"Well, I noticed that you had many yards of material, and I thought perhaps you might be using it to make clothes?"

"I am not making clothes," said Sebastian, looking up suddenly from his sewing machine. "Although I do that too. It is a much larger project than that."

Timothy wasn't making much progress, but still he persisted, with good spirits, in his inquiry.

"I might need some assistance, if you would be willing to help?" said the skunk, turning round on his little stool. "I have just received a commission to repair some sails for a schooner. Normally, I would have been able to manage on my own, you see, had it not been for the *other*….job… the one I am working on at present."

The skunk returned to his tapping, guiding the needle along long strips of canvas.

Timothy thought that attempting to get an explanation from a skunk was like trying to get juice from a pawpaw fruit!

"If you need help, I can call my chelonian family – they are near."

"I suppose you will need something in return?" said Sebastian.

"No, indeed not, Sir," said Timothy Trumble earnestly. "You can count on us for help."

"Then, have you heard the news?" Sebastian continued.

"You mean, about the delays in the brush clearing?"

"No, about the *Great Winged Bird*," said Sebastian, looking over rather large, square-rimmed glasses. "The otters informed me that the silver bird will fly over the woodland tomorrow and along the edge of the river. I must have the parasols ready. I will have to work all night."

"Oh," said Timothy, looking undaunted. "The

mosquitoes are probably bothering the humans. They like to do that."

"But this is not the *little* bird, the one we know," said Sebastian. "They have called out the Air Reserve this time. It's much more serious. We shall have to take cover!"

Timothy called in the other chelonians, and before long they were measuring, cutting, and carrying material to Sebastian for stitching. The group worked all night and made many pots of tea to help them stay awake. By dawn, they had made enough parasols for their woodland friends and families. Many who had their homes underground could retreat to the burrows and dens, but the fledglings were particularly in danger, as many of the nests were high in the trees.

The chelonians sent word to the other animals and alerted the birds. At six o'clock the next morning, the airlift squadron set out on their spraying mission. The animals watched furtively through binoculars for the sign, which would be given by the muskrats. The corvids, falcon and other species, high in the trees, awaited the alarm.

All of a sudden, the thrum-thrum of engines could be heard rumbling along the edge of the woodland beach, and the great silver bird appeared near the inlet. She was not the little single-engine flyer they were accustomed to. Indeed, this was the largest bird they had ever seen near the river. The peregrine falcons returned to the nest to protect their young, and the alarm rang out through the woodland: "PARASOLS UP!"

Everyone ducked into burrow, den and warren, beneath parasol, or under large leaves! Suddenly a very peculiar smell filled the animals' nostrils, made their eyes water and caused them to sneeze. It was some time before they could come out again, but slowly, gradually, they emerged, and around eight o'clock it was considered safe to go above ground or emerge from beneath parasols.

Off they went – corvids, falcons, tortoises, squirrels, foxes, muskrats and groundhogs – in a long line toward the skunk's burrow. Sebastian was in a deep sleep, of course, having worked so hard all night. When he awakened, he found a large thank you note, written in fine calligraphy by the chelonians, a basket filled with nuts and berries, and a small dish of sardines awaiting him. Sebastian emerged from the burrow, slowly, sampled some berries, and then looked around the see if there was anyone there. Behind the trees, he could see something moving, but as his eyesight was poor, he simply put on his glasses and sat down at the little sewing machine, pressing the pedal to begin his day's work.

"Shhhh!" said the animals, and then one of the squirrels whispered, "Go on Timothy!"

Timothy Trumble stepped forward, "Excuse me, Mr. Sebastian, we came to thank you for the parasols and for your diligence. All the woodland fledglings are well and the nests are dry. Everyone has come to thank you, except the raccoons and opossums, who are not yet back home from their voyage."

Sebastian removed his glasses and stepped forward. Dressed in a finely tailored red jacket with gold buttons, he put one leg forward and bowed in a very gentlemanly fashion. "I am at your service," he said, very quietly.

CHAPTER THIRTEEN
Powhatan Past

There was much merriment in the woodland, and the animals' concerns about their homes had temporarily been set aside. They anxiously awaited the return of their seafaring friends. Everyone wanted to hear the news of the journey and noted, with admiration, the seafarers' new fashions, for they wore odd-looking hats and strange sailor clothing. There was so much noise and chatter, giggling and oooohhs and aaaahhs that Cornelius had to intercept.

"While I understand your excitement and also wish to hear about the journey, I simply *must* ask you to be quiet. I have work to do! We can gather later to hear the high tales of the sea!" said the crow, rather crossly, for he was in need of some sleep.

Octavous, on the other hand, stood in the middle of the group, wearing his monocle so as not to miss anything! The raptor had time to listen to the stories, but then, he had not been up all night attending to the assembly of parasols. As the stories rang out through the woodland and the tales took on some additional drama with each telling, all the animals became so engrossed they almost forgot they had work to do in the west woodland.

"Just one more story, please, Sir," said Timothy Trumble to Obediah. "Just one more, Sir, before we begin our daily duties!"

"Silence!" announced Cornelius, once again. But

when the crow flew off to his tree, the incessant babble erupted at an even louder level, although the animals knew they were being very naughty.

And then an unexpected silence fell over the woodland. There was a loud rustle among the trees and a deep cracking of twigs and all of a sudden, two large figures appeared in the clearing. The animals gasped and held their breath, and it was not until Rachel charged in front of them that everyone relaxed. Dressed in a rather odd cook's hat and apron, which she had forgotten to remove, Rachel stepped forward.

"I would like to introduce two very special and kind friends," she said with a very excited expression, "Captain John Farley and young Master Tarquin from the schooner *Solaris*.

Captain Farley removed his cap, and Tarquin sat down so that he would not frighten the animals.

There was a loud reverberation of voices from tree to tree, burrow to burrow and perch to perch, and all the animals seemed to edge sideways and backwards to form a large mass of fur, feather and shell. The scene was so comical that Captain Farley and Tarquin began to laugh and, all at once, the animals joined in. Then, there was a grand chorus of voices:

"We're pleased to meet you Mister Captain and Master Tarquin!"

Cornelius had, by now, completely given up the hope of having a snooze. He longed for a quiet day, but it seemed one animal or another always interrupted him. Everyone summoned Cornelius when they needed advice, and when he tried to have a short snooze in the middle of the afternoon, a loud *B-O-O-M* would shake him off his perch! Cornelius knew that it was only the Yorktown cannon firing at three o'clock, but every day it surprised him, and each time he would be too late covering his ears!

Presenting an extensive and formidable wingspan, Octavious announced, "On behalf of all our woodland creatures, we extend our sincere gratitude for your kindness in caring for our opossums and raccoons." And then, removing his monocle, he added, "I hope they worked hard to atone for their earlier mischief!"

Captain Farley recounted the animals' hard work and how Rachel had saved Beauregard from being washed overboard in the storm!

Timothy Trumble then uttered a few words, quite out of time it was thought, but then he always spoke exactly from his heart. "Please Sir, Captain Farley," said the chelonian, "We have some peregrine falcon young, if you would like to see them?"

"I would love to see the falcon!" said Captain Farley, cheerfully. Then, he added, "If you have a falcon nest, it is good for the woodland."

"Why would that be so?" asked Grahame.

"The peregrine falcon is an endangered species. This may help us to save your homes."

And then Octavious spoke, "I am afraid this may not be enough. If the humans wish to build their homes on the land, what can we animals do? Removing undergrowth and many trees and shrubs will destroy our natural habitat."

Captain Farley sat down on a nearby log. "I will go with Tarquin tomorrow to visit the landowners, and we will see what may be possible."

Mukki then arrived with a strange concoction he had brewed for everyone. He called it *fragaria tea*, a drink that his Powhatan ancestors made from the leaves of wild strawberries. It was still a favorite at Muskrat Lodge, and Mukki had brewed a very large pot, but he feared there was not enough for everyone.

Mukki liked to compose a little verse on occasion. He thought it was a good way for the young muskrats to learn about the herbs he used for his cooking and medicines, so he came up with a short ditty, which the youngsters often sang:

All Will Gather for a Cup of Tea

Mint and Sage are efficacious, too.
Chamomile is curative for you.
We'll boil the herbs and mix them up with glee,
And all will gather for a cup of tea.

Now Lemonade and Syllabub are fine.
Scrumptious too, is Blackberry wine,
But the herbal infusion is unsurpassed to me,
And all will gather for some fresh mint tea.

Mukki worked steadily in his little apothecary shoppe, and the woodland animals were aware that he could drink up to twenty cups of tea at one sitting, which, it should be known, was rather too much of the gentle herb!

That night, Captain Farley, Tarquin and the crew sat on the deck of the *Solaris* just before sunset. The air was filled with the scent of lemon balm and wild bergamot, the green tree frog emitted a twang that sounded like a broken banjo string, and the great blue heron puttered around the shallow edge of the inlet, seeking a tasty morsel. A northern mockingbird sang loudly to its mate, trilling a merry song! Young raccoons, opossums and skunks gradually emerged from their burrows, and the call of the great horned owl could be heard for quite some distance, announcing that night had fallen in the woodland.

At dawn, Timothy Trumble set out for breakfast. As he made his way through a carpet of Virginia bluebells, an orange-yellow day lily smiled affectionately. Timothy Trumble smiled back and continued on his path toward a patch of red clover, while a downy woodpecker hammered away cheerfully at a tulip tree trunk, extracting some small insects for breakfast.

The woodland seemed alive and merry on that morning, and all the animals awaited news from Captain Farley and Tarquin, who had set out early for the development office.

Obediah and Rachel had gone to check the falcon's nest, and the crows kept watch at the edge of the woodland. All was quiet, and there were no signs of the humans. Not a single tree had been cut, nor brush removed. Grahame and the young groundhogs had been digging some new burrows, shoveling away and flinging bits and pieces out of the tunnels when suddenly they encountered something odd. Grahame cleaned the dust from his spectacles to take a closer look. In one of the burrows, he had found all sorts of strange objects and, as they were blocking his path, he had placed them in the little cart and pushed them out of the burrow so that he could look at them in the sunlight. There were small pieces of pottery, an odd-looking, curved clay object, some brown bowl-like objects, arrow heads, and a shiny piece that caused him to squint for a moment, as the sun bounced off the object and into his eyes. He held the object up and then saw that it was a piece of silver. Grahame did not know what the pieces were, so he placed them all back in the cart and took them to Octavious and Cornelius. While Octavious picked up each item and looked at it closely, Cornelius was suddenly smitten with the silver piece. The crow's eyes glazed over, and he became hypnotized by the article in front of him, so much so that Octavious had to clear his throat to bring Cornelius back from his trance.

"Ahem! Ahem!" said the osprey, stridently, peering out of his monocle at the crow.

Cornelius suddenly looked up. "Well, I was rather taken with the…."

"Yes! Yes!" replied Octavious. "However, we must first take the objects to Mukki for identification. I would appreciate it if nothing is removed from the cart until then." Cornelius had to forgo removing the silver piece, which he had hoped to add to his extensive collection.

CHAPTER FOURTEEN
Tea and Archaeology

Grahame and the groundhogs pulled the little cart quite some distance to Mukki's house. They were indeed tired and in need of some refreshment when they arrived. Mukki was working in his herb garden, concentrating on the collecting of nettles, when he heard the squeaking cart.

"Good Day," said the muskrat, wiping the loam off his paws. Then, he added, "I have some fresh fruit, if you would care for that."

"Oh, YES PLEASE!" answered the groundhogs.

Mukki then peered over the little fence. "May I know what you have in the cart?"

"Well," said Grahame, "We are hoping you can help us to answer that question, for we are all in quite a muddle!"

Mukki, who was always gracious, first saw to it that all the animals were fed and refreshed. He brought out dishes of fresh fruit and Indian corn bread, along with some nettle tea. The groundhogs tried not to show their dislike of the tea, but their faces betrayed them. While Mukki examined the articles they had carefully placed in the cart, the groundhogs threw the tea into a nearby bush, and when Mukki looked up to ask if they were enjoying their refreshment, they all smiled widely, holding their paws over the empty cups and said, "Yes, thank you, Mr. Mukki," very politely.

"What we seem to have here," said Mukki at length, "are some very ancient Powhatan artifacts."

The young groundhogs greeted Mukki's explanation with totally blank stares, but no one thought to ask the meaning of *artifact*. It seemed to be one of those strange words that you can't be bothered to look up, and that if you did look it up, you would soon forget it again. At least, that is how the young groundhogs felt about it.

Grahame then spoke, "An artifact is a *relic*. If you use the word at least three times, in three different sentences, then you will more likely remember it!"

"Oh," said one of the groundhogs, "Then, what is a relic, please, Sir?"

"A relic is an historical object," said Mukki, "and you have found some historical objects that may have been placed in the burrow long ago by my ancestors."

"Then, do we have to use three words, three times in nine sentences?" asked a very young groundhog.

"Well, yes, you do," said Grahame, "if you wish to remember all three words." Then he added, "I see you have been studying your math as well."

This pitter-pattering around with words and their meanings was suddenly interrupted by the sound of approaching wings. The teacups were tossed onto the ground, and the muskrats and groundhogs rumbled away for cover. They peered out from beneath a small fig tree.

Cornelius came in for a smooth landing near the herb garden. Octavious followed him, knickerbockers and talons in gear-down position. The raptor and the corvid scanned the area, and then, announced, "You can all come out – it's quite safe!"

Loud chatter then emanated from beneath the fig tree, and a collection of small snouts reappeared from the undergrowth.

The party stood to attention in front of the raptor.

"I bring the most excellent news," said Octavious, as Cornelius lifted a wing to quiet the chatter.

"Captain Farley and Master Tarquin returned this morning from the town. They held a meeting with the land trust officers and have placed our land in a trust that will protect our homes for a long time." Octavious then steadied his glance and observed each animal very seriously. "You must know that the peregrine falcons and their young will be accorded the most warm welcome, and we have been charged with protecting them and encouraging them to return each year to the same nest."

Every animal stood quite still, but none was able to speak, and it seemed that to break the silence after such news would be a slightly unwise thing to do.

The problem was, no one knew what a *land trust* meant. Cornelius stepped forward, and all the animals sat down quietly.

"Please, Mr. Cornelius," they requested, "can you tell us what a land trust means?" Cornelius challenged the animals to work the answer out for themselves. An enterprising squirrel said, "Well, Sir, does it mean to *trust* that the *land* will be looked after for the future? Rather like a safe harbor for a schooner?"

"You are on the right path," said Cornelius. "A land trust is something that protects lands and waters to help ensure the health and natural beauty of the area is conserved for our descendants. A land trust may also help to protect the watershed and prevent building on the land. We are so fortunate in Virginia to have many forested areas. Yet, every day, trees are cut down and forests lose more ground. We are all dependent upon each other, and all of nature works in a wheel of life." A young groundhog then asked, "But our woodland is so very small; who would be interested in such a small place as this, Sir?" Cornelius blinked thoughtfully, and then replied to the young animal. "Every place matters, be it a small woodland, an inlet, a stream or a tiny garden. For each place creates abundant life and helps to cool and clean our planet."

A young muskrat then stepped forward. Cornelius turned his head to the side and looked quizzically at the animal.

"Y-e-s?" he said.

"Well, Sir, our Uncle Mukki taught us a song about this very subject. We can sing it, i-i-i-i-f you like, Sir?"

Cornelius removed his spectacles. "*Another* song?" he said. Then he added, patiently, "Very well, then!"

Four young muskrats stood in a row and presented their piece:

Planet Earth

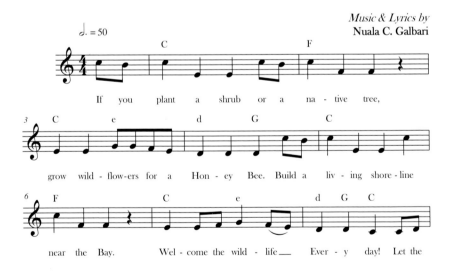

"Now," said Octavious at length, "that's enough singing and dancing for today. I have one more request."

Octavious then blinked a few times and stretched his wings. The young groundhogs and muskrats wished that Octavious would just hurry up and tell them what it was he wanted to convey. They became quite restless and would not stand still.

"No talking! Shhhhh!" cautioned Cornelius. The group once again fell quiet.

"It has been brought to my attention that an archaeologist will soon arrive to look at the artifacts found this morning by Grahame."

Cornelius then added, "If more such objects are found, the area near the groundhog burrows may become a focal point for a *dig*, which means we will see some human activity, but this time it will be friendly, and we need have no fear and must assist where we can."

"What's a dig, exactly?" interrupted a muskrat.

Octavious and Cornelius fell silent, and Mukki then

spoke. "A dig is, in a way, what Grahame was doing when he found some of the historical objects. A dig is a project to help uncover what life was like a long time ago. In addition to historical objects, archaeologists are also looking for plant remains, animal skeletons, or even weather patterns."

Mukki continued, "There is much to be learned about our Powhatan ancestors, and some of the objects found this morning may be very helpful in explaining the lives of our ancient families and how they lived."

"What else do they look for?" asked a young groundhog.

"They look for clues to the past, and then they put the clues together to form a story. It's rather like a broken pot. When you can pick up all the pieces and stick it back together with tree sap, then you can see what it looked like before it was broken."

"That seems like an awful lot of work to me, Sir," said a muskrat. "Is that rather like rebuilding our lodges after they are damaged – putting them back together the way they were?"

"Well," said Mukki, "you are going in the right direction! But you will learn more in the days to come."

"So really, Sir, it's a dig to uncover the past?"

"That's correct," said Mukki. "*Your* past! *Our* past!"

"And now," he said, "tea – I think!"

The groundhogs then made their strident apologies, but they were all suddenly very busy and had no time for more nettle tea!

Octavious and Cornelius returned to the clearing, and the muskrats gathered in a circle, ate cornbread and savored their favorite refreshment.

The animals were so excited, they babbled endlessly, until Mukki was obliged to send them out of the herb garden and back to their lodges.

"*Nummacha! Nummacha!*" he said. "Go home!"

His ears rang and buzzed for some time, until the noise finally subsided. Then, he poured another cup of tea and sat in his little garden chair at the edge of the riverbank, dozing off to the gentle sounds of the water and the 'coo-coo coo' of the mourning doves. It seemed to him that life in the woodland might continue and that perhaps he would be able to place some relics on the walls of his lodge. Musing on these things, Mukki fell asleep by the riverbank, his cup of tea still in his paws, and he dreamed the most wonderful dream.

CHAPTER FIFTEEN
Honored Visitors

Squadron Leader Rupert Gull had been out with the cadets since dawn. Had he been there, it would have been Cedric's first flight since the unfortunate ditching incident at Muskrat Lodge, and the young gull, eager to escape kitchen duty in the officers' mess, had to study his landing performance graphs and brush up on his weak areas. Cedric had been pouring over his flight manuals well into the night, when a gull's eyesight is not at its best, and members of his class had found him lying on his back in the little bunk, beak open wide, his webbed feet and wings hanging out from beneath the covers, with the flight manuals spread over the bed and his book light still on. Cedric had been too tired to even remove his kitchen cap, and the apron still bore the stains from last night's cooking.

"Wake up! Wake up!" said Rupert, shaking the poor bird gently. "Flight duty today! Eggs are served in the mess hall."

Slowly, Cedric's peepers opened and he peered, pink-eyed, at Rupert. And then it hit him. "Flight duty, Sir? Did you say, *flight duty?*"

"Yes!" replied Rupert, rolling his eyes. "And I'd take off that apron and cap, if I were you! Major Harwood's out this morning, and you had better be on your toes!"

Rupert and the cadets flew in formation over the York River and noticed a small group making their way in a rowing boat toward the inlet. It was just past eight o'clock when the little boat was pulled onto the sand, near the woodland. In an effort to learn who was in the boat, Cedric broke formation at the rear and landed nearby on the sand. Cornelius and Timothy welcomed the visitors.

"Welcome to our woodland, Chief Running Fox, Sir, and welcome, Mr. Howard, Sir," said Timothy Trumble, aiming a claw in the direction of Muskrat Lodge. "This way, if you please."

Octavious opened his wings slightly and bowed to the gentlemen. "We are honored by your visit."

Timothy Trumble led the way, and the Mattaponi chief and the archaeologist followed Octavious to the riverbank lodge, where Mukki was waiting. Cedric returned to the air and gave Rupert news of the special visitors to the lodge.

During the morning, Chief Running Fox, Mr. Howard and Mukki closely examined and discussed some of the fragments uncovered by the groundhogs. It was agreed by all that a dig in and around Groundhog Burrows would likely reveal more historical objects from the Eastern Woodland Indian period, and the knowledge gained would be most valuable to both the humans and the animals.

Timothy Trumble then posed a question. "Could we tortoises be of any help at all, Sir? I mean, we are very good at digging, you see."

Mr. Howard smiled and spoke gently to the chelonian. "Indeed you might, Timothy," he said, "I am sure we can put you to work."

While the gentlemen were discussing the site to be considered for the dig, Mukki had quietly slipped away with the cartload of historical objects. He moved silently into his muskrat cottage, where he unloaded the cart. He wrapped the items carefully in some muslin cloth that

Sebastian had given him. Then he placed the clay pipe, the coins, the arrowhead and the pottery fragments, together with some animal bones in a small trunk that he used as a tea table. There, the objects would be safe until the archaeologists returned.

While Mukki held counsel with Chief Running Fox and Mr. Howard, the animals became very excited about the prospect of working on the dig with the archaeologists, for there was much to learn on all sides. The animals would learn about their Powhatan past, the humans would learn about the history of the area, and perhaps best of all, the animals and the humans could learn about each other and how they could live together and share their land.

Mukki had picked some wild strawberries, which he offered to his guests. Chewing merrily on a strawberry, Timothy Trumble asked Mr. Howard, "What is to become of the large, open field, Sir? I mean, the field that lies to the west of the woodland, behind the Indian grass. I do so love to putter in the grasses, Sir! The songbirds like the seeds and plants, and Mr. Mukki likes to dry the flowers."

Fearing that Timothy Trumble would *never* stop talking unless he was interrupted, Mukki picked up the talking stick and waved it gently. Timothy then opened his mouth wide, but no sound emanated from it.

Just as Mr. Howard was about to answer Timothy Trumble's question, a sudden rush of sound came rapidly through the woodland, and before they knew it, Mukki, Timothy and their guests were surrounded by raccoons and opossums, the animals quite frenzied and out of breath!

"Oh, Mr. Mukki," cried an opossum joyfully, "It's true! The news is true! Mister Captain Farley just sent word with the gulls that our land has been placed in a trust; he says it's called The Wicomico Land Trust."

Another opossum then put in, "Yes, Sir. Mister Captain Farley has purchased the forty acres of woodland and also the field. He will build a small cottage in the big field, along with some stables and paddocks for his horses, but the thirty-five acres of woodland that comprises our home will remain in his family's trust and will be preserved as a natural wildlife habitat."

Rachel then arrived, took off her cook's hat and threw it high into the air! "Oh glorious old home, oh lovely, fair land!" she said, rather loudly! And everyone joined in the chorus.

Octavious and the gulls then arrived from the river.

The raptor announced, "Tomorrow night, there will be a grand celebration! The gulls will send word throughout the river and Bay. Timothy and the other chelonians will carry the news to all the woodland animals. I will duly inform the peregrine falcon and the corvids!" Then, looking through his monocle, Octavious said, "Oh, what a night we'll have! Wear your very finest tailored clothing, for tomorrow we'll dance and sing and feast!" And all the paws, claws and wings went up in the air, and all the animals shouted, Huzzah! Huzzah!

The Venerable Red Oak

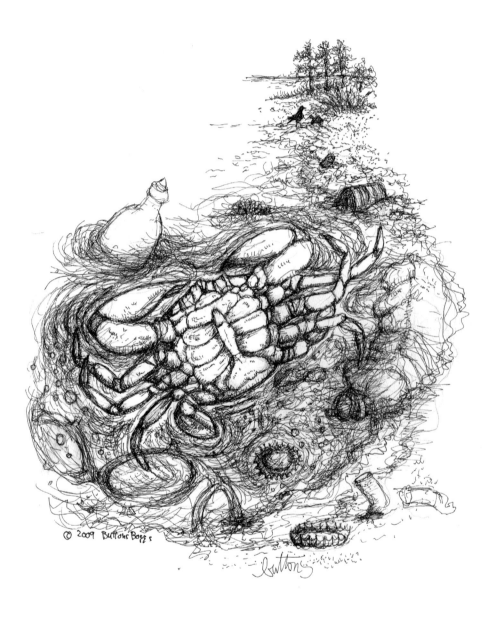

CHAPTER SIXTEEN
Right of Passage

Timothy Trumble and Cornelius arose very early the next morning, for there was much work to be done in and around the woodland, and the clearing had to be prepared for the evening's celebration. The two friends worked methodically around the little beach and called the otters and the muskrats in to help clean the inlet, for their honored guests would arrive by boat, and they hoped to welcome them with a tidy beach and woodland. While Timothy and Cornelius worked at the edge of the water, picking up debris, a small ripple of water suddenly washed something up on the beach, a little way in front of them. As they approached the area they found an old friend, Bertie the blue crab, lying upside down at the edge of the water. Timothy and Cornelius stood very quietly, watching Bertie floating in and out of the water.

"What do you think happened, Mr. Cornelius?" asked Timothy, wiping a tear from his eye.

"I don't know, Timothy, but I don't see any physical injury. Perhaps it was just Bertie's time. You know their species does not live very long, compared to us corvids, and certainly not compared to chelonians."

"But…but…Bertie wasn't even two years old, Sir," blubbered Timothy through his tears. "It seems to me that he should have lived longer."

"He may have taken ill, my young friend," said

Cornelius, placing a wingtip on the tortoise's shell. "Perhaps he was trying to come home to his family and friends, and the tide brought him here."

"Oh, Sir," said Timothy, with a heavy heart, "what can we do?"

"Bertie was our friend," said Cornelius. "We will bury him at the edge of the woodland, near the water, where he will always be home and near us."

"Oh yes, Sir," said Timothy, "indeed we must do that." And then he added, "I am sorry I cried, Sir."

"Your tears are blessings that the angels will carry to Bertie. He will know we are here."

The two friends stood quietly together for a moment, then they gently lifted Bertie out of the water and placed him on the sand.

"Sometimes, Sir," said Timothy Trumble, "you wonder if you make a difference in the lives of others; you wonder if you do enough to help."

"We all make a difference, Timothy," said the corvid, "even though we may not always know it. It can be the smallest token, like a cheerful word when someone is feeling sad, or a warm hug when another animal is cold. At other times, we give more, such as caring for someone who is sick, or one who is feeling lonely. Each day, it is good to strive to make someone feel better or happier, or to help them make a wiser decision."

"But we couldn't save poor Bertie, Mr. Cornelius, Sir. We couldn't do that."

"No, Timothy, but we can help his family. There is always something you can do, if you act with a kind heart."

"Do you think that is why we are here in the first place, Sir, to love and to care for others?"

"I think you are a very wise, young tortoise, Timothy Trumble! Our people have always taught that you should leave the world a little better than you found it."

"So even if you cannot fly, Sir, your heart and spirit can reach great heights?"

"That is the essence of life, Timothy," said the corvid.

The otters and muskrats swam in silently to the beach, and the raccoons and opossums brought the woodland animals to the service for Bertie. All stood without a word looking to the inlet and the river. The brackish water lay flat and lifeless in the mid-morning heat, and sludge had floated to the edge of the beach. It just seemed to the animals that the water was murkier than it used to be. "What can we do, Mr. Mukki, to help keep our woodland clean and our waters fresh?" asked Timothy Trumble in earnest. Mukki, who was mixing some herbs in a little bowl, answered, "Our people can teach the humans to live in harmony with the land and the water, if they seek the knowledge."

After a little while, the animals prepared a small grave for Bertie under a shade tree near the water. Then they joined paws, claws and flippers and sang a little song together:

Victus Astrum

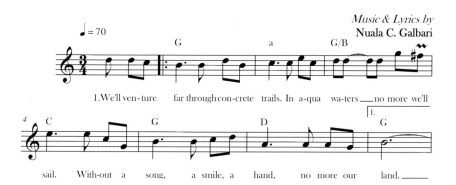

Music & Lyrics by
Nuala C. Galbari

Right of Passage

2. The Blue Crab weeps, the Tree Frog too,
No longer home that we once knew
For it is written in the sand--
No more our land.

The quiet was suddenly broken by the sound of something crashing through the trees. There followed a loud *"WHOOPS!"* and then an *"EE-OW"* and finally a *"Well, of all the...OUCH!"* Then, all fell silent, as the animals waited for any further exclamations.

"You impractical, illogical gull!" said Rupert, landing smoothly on the beach.

Rupert and the animals tiptoed around the trunk of an aged red oak to find Cedric attempting to free himself from some Virginia creeper in which he had become entangled!

"How on earth do you expect to pass your flight test this afternoon, Cedric?" asked Rupert, freeing the bird from the plant while shaking his head in disbelief! "Injuring yourself beforehand is *possibly not* the best idea!"

"Well, you see, Sir, I was just trying one more water landing before my test, but I think I encountered low level wind shear on the horizontal plane."

"Wind shear, indeed!" said Rupert. "Alright, Cedric – back to base! Flight test at 1400 hours -- and remember your magnetic bearings for autumn migration!"

Cedric shook himself off and followed his squadron leader.

"Goodbye, Cedric!" said the animals. "Good luck with your test!"

For most of the afternoon, the animals decorated the woodland, picking ornamental grasses and wildflowers and gathering berries, seeds, and fruit. Mukki spent hours preparing herbal teas, and Rachel baked many loaves of cornbread. The corvids dropped invitations into all the nests, while the chelonians and opossums cleared some space for a dance floor. The raccoons brought in some logs for the musicians.

"Mr. Octavious, Sir," said Timothy Trumble, suddenly interrupting the raptor during his afternoon nap.

"*Yes* – Timothy?"

"Only, I was just wondering, well, the humans cannot sit on the woodland floor, probably. Perhaps we will need some large logs for their comfort, Sir?"

The raptor sighed, "Timothy, you are quite right. We didn't consider that. Indeed we must

Right of Passage

provide larger logs."

Before long, a team of raccoons had wrapped Virginia creeper around some larger logs and used it as a harness to pull the logs into the clearing. With everything ready for the celebration, the animals returned to their burrows, perches and dens to have an afternoon nap.

The *Solaris* crewmembers were also busy with preparations for their forthcoming trip. Sebastian had delivered the repaired canvas and the supplies had been procured for their journey. Captain Farley had recruited some new crewmembers and, with Obediah's help, had spent the past few days training them in their duties. Obediah was standing on deck when he suddenly heard a loud opossum chorus calling, "Mr. Obediah! Mr. Obediah, Sir! Please come quickly!"

Obediah jumped down onto the jetty and followed the opossums, who ran at some pace toward the west woodland.

"Where are we going?" he asked. "Why are you in such a hurry?"

The opossums would not answer but merely edged Obediah onward until they reached the Indian grass.

Tarquin was waiting in the paddock, and the opossums excitedly jumped through the new fencing and pointed to the stable.

When Obediah reached the fence, he looked into the stable and heard a whinnying coming from within!

"Why, it's Penelope!" he shouted with great cheer. "Penelope has come to live beside our woodland!"

A few minutes later, Rachel came barreling through the woods and ran toward the stable. She was squealing with excitement!

Tarquin opened the stable door, and Penelope cantered out to the paddock, her tail swishing around merrily. She kicked up her rear hooves with delight and then cantered over to Obediah and Rachel, who danced with glee! "We've come to live here now, in our new stables!

"Tarquin said we will spend the autumn, winter and spring here and then go to Assateague during the summers! Isn't it just too exciting?" Before anyone could answer, Penelope took off again at a brisk canter. A few minutes later, another painted pony emerged from the stable. "I thought you would like to meet Penelope's mother!" said Tarquin, with a huge smile.

Rachel and Obediah were so thrilled at seeing Penelope and her mother, they almost forgot they had work to do!

At sunset on that late summer's day, the katydids sang their piercing chorus in the woodland, and all the animals gathered in celebration of their home. Sebastian had tailored some very fine clothes for the evening, and his small paws were quite sore from having worked for several nights at the sewing machine. There was a great feast laid out, plenty of tea and music and dancing to lift the spirits high. Obediah, dressed in a smart nautical outfit, danced a sailor's jig while the opossums, squirrels, raccoons and foxes played fiddles, flutes and drums. Everyone joined in the dancing, and it was genuinely felt that the dance floor could have been a little larger to accommodate the guests!

Tarquin brought Penelope and her mother to the edge of the woodland, and even the peregrine falcon parents attended the gathering, while keeping a watchful eye on their young. Timothy Trumble and Cornelius ensured that everyone had enough to eat and drink, and Octavious sat with the honored guests: Captain Farley, Tarquin, Chief Running Fox and Mr. Howard. It wasn't long before some additional guests arrived: Rupert and the young cadets, all of whom passed their flight test, including Cedric, joined the gathering with great enthusiasm! Sebastian sat on a small log at the edge of the woodland, but even he joined in with the singing. Naturally, he was dressed in a very smart waistcoat and shirt, and the lady skunks were all quite giggly and hoped he would ask them to dance.

When the music stopped, Octavious stood in the center of the clearing.

"Tonight," he said, very regally, "I am honored to celebrate our woodland! Let us all go forward with love and hope. Let us ensure we work together for the good of the land and teach our young to care for our woodland, our rivers and our Bay, and for all species."

There was a very loud applause, and then Octavious removed his monocle. "And now! Mr. Mukki has written a minuet. I would like to see *everyone* dancing!"

"Oh, what a brilliant, magical night this is, Mr. Cornelius, Sir!" said Timothy Trumble. "But I think I have had a little too much of Mr. Mukki's tea!"

Cornelius placed a wingtip on Timothy's head, and then he removed his spectacles. "Come along, Timothy," he said. "I think it's time for us to join in the dance!"

As the music played, all the animals learned new steps, while following Mr. Mukki's lead, of course! A chorus rang out in the woodland. Cornelius noted that, on this occasion at least, *almost* everyone sang in tune.

Muskrat Minuet

2. There are songs and dances on this summer's night
And a banquet so divine.
With a merry step, we dance a minuet
In our tailored clothes so fine!

Chorus:
Celebrate our woodland
The flowers and fauna there.
Praise our bounteous river,
Virginia, oh so fair!

3. Will you join us in our Muskrat Minuet?
Let the woods ring out the cheer.
You can dance with species you have never met.
Glorious summer time is here!

Chorus

The next morning at dawn, while the animals slept, Obediah sat on the jetty, watching the *Solaris* pull gently on her ropes. It was time for the schooner to depart, and she eagerly awaited her freedom. Obediah had not gone to bed and had watched the sun slowly awaken, casting a warm glow over the river. He lifted his snout and sampled the gentle, salty breeze from the Bay, while the *Solaris* creaked softly in her moorings. A tinge of autumn was in the air. Obediah set down his cup of tea and ran to his burrow; he found a pen and some paper and began writing.

A rooster crowed and awakened many of the animals, whose legs were quite sore from the previous night's dancing. As Timothy passed Obediah's burrow, he noticed a sign on the door and drew closer to read it.

The little note said, quite simply, "Gone Sailing! Back soon."

Then he heard laughter emanating from the edge of the woods. Timothy went over to the Indian grass to see what was causing the commotion. He found Octavious, Cornelius, Penelope, and some of the opossums gathered in a group beside the paddock. Tarquin was with them. "Oh, good morning, Mr. Octavious, Sir," said Timothy politely. "Good morning, Master Tarquin, Sir. I was just passing, and I heard the merriment. I was looking for Mr. Obediah, you see."

"Oh, it's just far too funny!" said Penelope. And the gathering once again dissolved into laughter. "You see," said Penelope, shaking her head, "Mr. Obediah packed his bags this morning and sailed with the *Solaris*." Penelope then rolled over in the grass, kicking her legs in the air.

"Oh, then, have they sailed to Assateague?" asked Timothy.

Octavious removed his monocle and wiped a tear of laughter from his eye. "The *Solaris* is *not* going to Assateague Island, Timothy, she's sailing to Antigua. Obediah has gone to the Caribbean for the winter, but he doesn't yet know it! He boarded the schooner early this morning, after a long night studying his notes on celestial navigation. The animal ate some porridge for breakfast

and must have fallen asleep in his bunk."

"Oh, heavens!" said Timothy with a worried expression. "Poor Mr. Obediah!"

"*Fortunate* Mr. Obediah, I would say, young Timothy!" said Cornelius. "Just think of the stories he will tell us when he returns in the spring. Think what adventures he will have sailing to the Windward Islands!"

Octavious extended his wings fully. "Well, I will be wintering in the Caribbean myself, so I can closely observe our marsupial mariner."

What none of the animals knew was that Rachel had run down the jetty, at the last minute, and jumped onto the *Solaris*. After all, they could not have sailed without their assistant cook, and *someone* had to take care of that seafaring opossum!

THE WOODS OF WICOMICO
WORD LIST

A
abnormalities
abundant
a capella
accorded
aquatic
acquired
adjacent
aerobatic
airwaves
altitude
amends
amidships
amiss
amphibian
ample
ancestors
ancient
animated
anticipation
antics
apothecary
apprehensive
aqua
archaeology
artifacts
assemble
assigned
atone
atonal
attendant
authoritative
awry
azure

B
babbling
beam (of a ship)
billowed
boundary
bounteous
bow (of a ship)
bowed
brackish
briskly
bulkhead
burrow

C

cacophony
calligraphy
cantered
celestial
clamor
collided
colony
comestibles
commotion
commission
concoction
confront
conserved
contemplated
convene
convey
council
counsel
courteously
cumulonimbus

D

debris
decisive
defiant
dejectedly
delectable
descendants
desist
detract
dig
dignity

dilemma
diligence
diminutive
discerned
dismayed
dispatches
dispute
dissolved
distracted
ditching
dwelling

E

eagerly
earnestly
efficacious
emitted
endangered
engrossed
enlist
entangled
enterprising
enthrall
entourage
entrenched
expending
examined
extensive
extracting

Word List

F
fauna
feat
fetlocks
filly
fledgling
focal
foresail
formation
formidable
forested
fragments
frenzied
frolic
furrowed
furtively

G
galley
genus
gesturing
giddily
glazed
grave (as in serious)
grounded

H
habitat
halyards
harmony
haunches
harried

heeled
helm
horizontal
hue
humidity
hypnotized

I
illogical
immense
imperceptibly
impish
implored
inclement
indulged
industrious
inlet
instinctively
insubordination
intently
intercept

J
jarring
jetty
jig
journeyed

K
keel (of a ship)
kneaded

knickerbockers
knots

L
languid
lattice
leeward
legend
loam
lugger
lurched

M
magnetic
mainsail
mammal
mariner
marsupial
medley
melee
menacing
methodically
minuet
mischievous
mizzen
monocle
moorings
morsel
muslin
muted

N
navigated
nautical
nest
nimbly
noble
nonchalantly
notable
nourish
nuzzled

O
obstinately
optimistically
ornamental
overindulgence

P
paddock
palette
pamphlets
parallel
parasols
partial
prevailing
peevish
perceive
perched
perplexed
petulant
pleaded
plight

Word List

portend
posse
precociously
proclaimed
procured
puttering

Q
quizzical

R
rationing
ratlines
ravines
reconvene
reef
refrain
regally
relic
reptile
retorted
revenge
reverberated

S
scanned
scuttled
scrumptious
seafaring
serenaded
serene

shanties
skeletons
slinking
sludge
slumped
smitten
snootily
sojourn
solemn
squadron
steadied
strains
strategy
stratus
strident
striking
stubbornly
sturdily
subsided
summoned
surveying
sway
swell (of the Bay or Ocean)
symbiosis

T
tagging
talons
tempest
tempestuous
thermals
topsails
trance

trilling
trundled
tutelage
twang

U
undaunted
undergrowth
unsurpassed
updraft

V
variable
velocity
venerable
ventured
veritable
vigil
vigilant
vigor
vivacity
volatile

W
wafted
warren
watershed
whinnying
windward

Z
zigzagged

LATIN GLOSSARY

Fauna	**Genus and Species**
blue crab	*Callinectes sapidus*
blue jay	*Cyanocitta cristata*
bottlenosed dolphins	*Tursiops truncatus*
cat	*Felis silvestris catus*
coyote	*Canis latrans*
downy woodpecker	*Picoides pubescens*
eastern gray squirrel	*Sciurus carolinensis*
fish crow	*Corvus ossifragus*
great horned owl	*Bubo virginianus*
green treefrog	*Hyla cinerea*
groundhog	*Marmota monax*
katydids	*Tettigoniidae*
laughing gull	*Leucophaeus atricilla*
meadow vole	*Microtus pennsylvanicus*
mourning dove	*Zenaida macroura*
muskrat	*Ondatra zibethicus*
northern mockingbird	*Mimus polyglottos*
osprey	*Pandion haliaetus*
painted ponies	*Equus caballus*
peregrine falcon	*Falco peregrinus*
piping plover	*Charadrius melodus*

raccoon	*Procyon lotor*
red fox	*Vulpes vulpes*
ring-billed gulls	*Larus delewarensis*
skunk	*Mephitis mephitis*
tortoise (Eastern Box Turtle)	*Terrapene c. carolina*
Virginia opossum	*Didelphis virginiana*

LATIN GLOSSARY

Flora	**Genus and Species**
bayberry	*Myrica pensylvanica*
black walnut tree	*Juglans nigra*
clover	*Trifolium*
daylily	*Hemerocallis*
dandelion	*Taraxacum*
Indian grass	*Sorghastrum nutans*
lemon balm	*Melissa officinalis*
loblolly pines	*Pinus taeda*
northern red oak tree	*Quercus rubra*
pawpaw	*Asimina triloba*
sassafras	*Sassafras albidum*
sweetgum tree	*Liquidambar styraciflua*
tulip tree	*Liriodendron tulipifera*
Virginia bluebell	*Mertensia virginica*
Virginia creeper	*Parthenocissus quinquefolia*
wild bergamot	*Monarda fistulosa*
wild strawberry	*Fragaria virginiana*

Nuala Galbari was born in Belfast, Northern Ireland, the daughter of a Royal Navy Lieutenant-Commander. She studied hospitality management at the Belfast College of Business Studies and later moved to London to pursue a career in aviation. After attending Normandale College and the Minnesota School of Business, she joined the editorial staff of a Minnesota advertising agency. She has contributed articles and stories to *Pleasant Living* magazine, and writes regularly for *Airways* magazine. Nuala is a member of the Authors Guild and the Society of Children's Book Writers and Illustrators (SCBWI). She lives in Virginia.

Buttons Boggs is an illustrator, portrait painter, muralist, sculptor, writer and book artist. She has been an artist and writer-in-residence in King William County, Petersburg, Norfolk, Virginia Beach and Richmond, Virginia schools. She is the author and illustrator of *Noah and the Ark as Told by Unkle Ernie*. She has also illustrated *Lily of St. Lukes: The Blessing of the Animals*, written by Fran Olsen, *River Rats*, written by Ralph Christopher, and *The Monarch's Feast*, from the family and friends of the Mary Munford School. She has a daughter, Belle, son, Sky, and son-in-law, Richard. She lives in beautiful downtown Walkerton, Virginia.